FROM HELL
to High Waters

WILLIAM THOMAS

BALBOA
PRESS

A DIVISION OF HAY HOUSE

Balboa Press books may be ordered through booksellers or by contacting:

Balboa Press
A Division of Hay House
1663 Liberty Drive
Bloomington, IN 47403
www.balboapress.com
1-(877) 407-4847

ISBN: 978-1-4525-3275-2 (sc)
ISBN: 978-1-4525-3277-6 (hc)
ISBN: 978-1-4525-3276-9 (e)

Library of Congress Control Number: 2011901745

Printed in the United States of America

Balboa Press rev. date: 4/5/2011

To my wife Frances

She has been and always will be my inspiration, my love

You are from my Christmas attic because having you
in my life every day is a gift from God

Thank you to my family, my son Thomas, my daughter
Elizabeth, my grandson D.J., and my granddaughter Maria

INTRODUCTION

We make choices every day of our lives, and every one of those choices affects the people we love and those who love us. How many times have you said or heard someone else say, "I can't"?

When I was in junior high school, my grandfather told me, *"Can't is just another word for won't."* I'm not referring to those who have been stricken with a sickness or some other unfortunate incident that prevents them from doing certain things. I'm simply saying that you cannot let that word rule your life. Don't let anyone or anything take you down. I needed to take responsibility and accountability for my choices and decisions, but I refused to do that because I did not have control of my life. I allowed that word *can't* to be my choice; as a result, I had to learn the hard way.

When I was a youngster, we had no counseling as we have today. In fact, the motto back in my day was: Children should be seen and not heard. How true that was. A child had no say and no right to an opinion, thought or feeling. I ended up creating a hell for myself and for those I loved. Finding the entrance to it was easy with the help of people who said they were my friends. I was in a world of illusion and disillusion, torture and agony, for many years.

I desperately tried to reach out to be understood, accepted, and validated by others, but that desperation clouded my thinking and judgment. I wound up grabbing on to individuals who I thought would accept me for who I was.

I am writing this book to you, the readers, in hopes that somehow a word or a sentence contained in it will help you or someone you know find an exit from hell and the entrance to high waters.

CHAPTER I

MY CHILDHOOD

I came into this world the last of three children, born into a family of blue-collar, low-income working people. I grew up on the streets in Astoria, New York, and my parents divorced. I don't know exactly when my dad left, but my mom told me I was just a baby. I was sent to live with my grandparents when I was eight months old. My mom and brother moved in about a year later. My brother Cliff was eighteen months older than me. We had an older sister, Irene, who we wouldn't know existed until fourteen years later.

The neighborhood where my grandparents lived was made up of Irish, Italian, German, Polish, Greek, and Jewish people. They were all hardworking people. There were about twelve families on our block, almost all with children. I remember how all the kids on the block would always hang out together, playing games like tag and hide-and-goseek. On Halloween, we would go trick-or-treating in our homemade customs. Some of the kids would dress up like hobos carrying a stick with a bundle tied to it and the end of it over their shoulder while wearing their fathers' torn-up old clothes. Their parents would take a cork and burn it with a match until the cork got black and then rub it on their kids' faces to give the appearance of dirt. Of course, the girls would dress up in their moms' clothes and make-up, except for Rose. She was the tomboy of the block, and she would usually dress as a bum, a ghost, or a skeleton, but never in a dress—no matter what kind.

The woman who lived next door to us was Mrs. Solana. She had three grown children: Betty, Kathy, and John, who was the youngest. I used to look up to him. He could and would play the piano and saxophone like I had never heard before. When he got discharged from the military, I would spend time over at his house and he would teach me how to play the piano. I would sit next to him on the bench and watch him play. Then he would show me the keys to touch. He showed me how to play the saxophone. I tried to play it, but it seemed bigger than me. Besides, I couldn't blow that hard. John was a great guy. He was never too busy for me.

One Halloween, I asked him if I could wear his uniform. The pants had to be taken up and the waist taken in, but still, even though it was kind of big, I thought it looked good. He even let me wear some of his medals he had earned: a sharpshooter's medal and a good conduct medal.

After the Halloween party, I gave him back the uniform. As he took off the medals, he handed me his sharpshooter's medal and said, "I want you to have this."

My mouth dropped and I was in awe. "You're kidding me," I said.

"No" he said. "It's yours to keep," he insisted.

I threw my arms around him. "Thanks, John, this is great.

About two weeks later, John had gotten real sick, and one day his temperature got so high that he dropped dead on the street. He had pneumonia and didn't even know it. He was twenty-seven years old.

Everyone in the neighborhood was shocked. He was so well liked. He had only been married three weeks. His wife came up to me outside the funeral home and told me how much he liked me. I cried so hard that day. It was like I lost my big brother. His mom died from a broken heart two weeks after him. They said his death was too much for her. Plus, she wasn't in the best of health herself.

I remember there were times when John would help some of us kids build our own scooters out of wood. We usually used a long piece of wood called a two-by-four, meaning the wood was two inches thick and four inches wide. We would go to the local fruit store and get an empty fruit box and nail that to the two-by-four, and to make the handles we would use two pieces of wood and nail them to the fruit box. We also made our own skateboards before they were ever given that name. We would take a two-by-four piece of wood, nail it to our skates, and then jump on it and ride. Not as fancy as the ones today, but it was to us.

The families on our block were good people for the most part. I was the second youngest on the block; the youngest was a girl name Jan, who the kids used to call *baby Jan*. She

3

was a plump, short girl with dark black hair and big dimples. She had a big crush on me, and it used to drive me crazy. Every time one of the parents would get all the kids together for a picture, they would stand her next to me. And I would make ugly faces when they took the picture. It was my way of letting them know I could not stand being next to her. She was about a year younger than me; however, I must admit I did think she was cute. But I couldn't tell her that because of the other kids. They would've teased me to no end. They were teasing me enough already, saying things like "Jan likes William " over and over every time she would come out to play with us.

One summer day, baby Jan asked me to come over to her house and go into her pool with her. It was a little rubber pool, which held about eight inches of water, but when you're six years old that seems deep enough. I knew if the rest of the kids found out that I went over there I'd never live it down. So, one early Saturday morning, I climbed over the two fences that separated our yards and went to meet baby Jan in her pool. We were in the pool splashing and actually having fun when we both decided to play a game. I asked her if she wanted to play doctor she said yes. She had a Popsicle stick and said we could use it like the real doctors. So I took the stick and told her to open her mouth, and I put the stick on her tongue and said, "Say ahhh." She let out a big sound and we both giggled. I was actually having fun with her.

Then she said, "Let's see each other's pee pee. Okay, you can touch mine with the stick." So I took the stick and on the outside of her bathing suit I put the stick down by her privates and said to her, "Say ahhh." Just about that time her mother came out, a tall, big woman. When she saw us, she yelled at me to get out of the pool. I must've turned solid white because my little heart was beating so fast at the moment. I jumped up and jumped over her backyard fence into the next yard. I started to climb the fence between my yard and the one I was in when the neighbor's dog Queeny came running after me. I screamed as I climbed the fence, thinking, *I hope I make it over in time!* When Queeny latched onto my bathing suit, I noticed the dog was trying to pull it down while I was thinking, *This dog's going to eat me!*

I fought with all my might, and finally she let go and over the fence I went. I hit the ground like a ton of bricks but still got up and ran into the house huffing and puffing. My grandmother said, "Come here. You look so pale. Do you feel all right?"

"Yes, Grammy, I'm fine."

About five minutes later, baby Jan 's mother came to the door and told my mother what we were doing in the pool. My mom came storming into the kitchen and beat the shit out of me while screaming and calling me a dirty, filthy boy. I thought she was going to kill me. My grandmother had to yell at her to stop.

My grandmother took me, washed me up, and held me close to her, saying, "It's okay." I felt safe with her. I had two wonderful grandparents who taught me what love was all about. If it wasn't for them, I don't think I would have known the meaning of the word.

My grandfather was a short, partially bald-headed man with a muscular build. He was born and raised in one of the toughest neighborhoods in the five boroughs: the South Bronx. For some reason, I never called him Grandpa. I just used to call him by his name: Frankie. It was like we had this incredible friendship, but I always knew inside that he was my grandfather and a real dad to me, since my real dad left us. My grandmother used to tell me stories about my grandfather when he was young. He used to work here and there for a guy named Lucky Lucci back then. Lucky Lucci was in the mob, better known to some people as the mafia. My grandmother wouldn't tell me everything he did for the mob, just that he delivered booze during the Prohibition days. I remember there were times when a man who was known as Willie the Book would come to our house to see my grandfather and they would go down to the cellar and be there for hours. I don't know what they talked about, but, every time when they were finished, on his way out the door Willie would throw my brother and me a five-dollar bill. That was a lot of money back then. It would buy us at least a week's worth of candy.

My grandfather was Italian and my grandmother was English. My grandmother was born and raised in Bermuda. She came to the United States when she was in her teens. She was a short, stocky woman with a big heart and skin as clear as glass. She was like a grandmother to every kid on the block. All the kids called her Grammy. I remember if one of the kids on the block was going home after playing at our house, she would wash his or her face and comb his or her hair and say, "You can't go home with dirt on your face and your hair messed up." She was like the law of the block. If Grammy said to *do it*, the parents would tell their kids to do what she told them and no questions were asked. But every kid on the block loved her. She was so kind.

Whenever summertime came, about nine or ten of us would pile into my grandfather's pick-up and head for Coney

Island beach, where we would spend the whole day. We would have empty wooden fruit boxes full of sandwiches and fruit. I sometimes would stand on the beach, where the water would flow over my feet, look across the ocean, and wonder what was on the other side or what it would be like to swim the English Channel. The ocean seemed to be my spiritual place; just the sounds of the waves made me feel good inside. When I would go into the ocean, it was like another world. I felt safe there. I didn't know it then, but the ocean would one day become an important part of my life.

My mom was a very hardworking woman who worked in a factory not far from our house. My relationship with my mom was not a good one. I believe to this day that she was a very depressed woman and possibly manic. She had very bad mood swings, which I think contributed to her way of doing and saying things. There were times she was very abusive toward me, both physically and mentally. This usually occurred when she drank. She drank very heavily on the weekends, just about every Friday and Saturday either at home or at a place called Terry's Bar and Grill. She had a bad temper and was quick with it.

My mom's sister, my aunt Emily, was also a heavy drinker as was her husband, my uncle Carl. They had two girls: Priscilla and Kelly. Those poor kids had it just as rough in their house as it was in ours. Priscilla and Kelly were older than my brother and me and they used to baby sit my brother and me. Those girls were so beautiful, and I remember I had the biggest crush on Priscilla. She had long blond hair and blue eyes and I thought for sure I was going to marry her someday. Every time she would have a boyfriend, I would dislike him because I felt he was taking her from me. She would call me *Giggles* because I would laugh a lot. Those girls had it just as rough growing up as we did living in an abusive household.

My uncle was very abusive toward my aunt; he would beat her to no end. There were times he would break her arm and punch her in her face, but, for some strange reason, she stayed with him. There were few divorces in those days, and *domestic violence* was unheard of. If the cops were called, they would tell the woman just to behave and keep her mouth shut and everything would be all right.

It seems both my mom and my aunt just seemed to be attracted to abusive situations. I know my mom could be abusive, but my aunt never was. There were times when my aunt would come over on a Friday night and I knew that meant that she and my mom would get into an altercation. I would hear them in the early hours of the morning, which usually woke me up out of a sound sleep. I was about five years old. I could hear the arguing and I could feel my heart beating faster and faster. When I would ask them to quit fighting, my mother would hit me and send me back to bed. I recall one time that I came out of my bedroom to find the refrigerator covered in blood. That had me screaming. I dreaded the weekends knowing full well what was on the agenda. I would say, "Mom, no fighting." In my heart I know that there would be fighting.

Those fights went on for years. Sometimes my mom would drink at the local pub and bring her boyfriend home and, sure enough, after a few hours of drinking in the house they would get into a physical altercation and my grandparents would have to break them up, putting my mom's boyfriend out of the house. My mom seemed to always get into physical confrontations, either with her boyfriend or my aunt, and this went on throughout most of my childhood.

On most Sundays, my brother and I would spend it at the Terry's Bar and Grill up from our house. Just about everyone in the neighborhood went there. My brother and I would get money from the people who drank too much and buy candy. I think that's why we spent so much time there. My mom's boyfriend, who worked as a bartender at Terry's on the weekends, was a tall blond-haired guy with a hot temper. He had a reputation for being tough and no one to mess with. He also worked for the city as a cashier in a booth selling train tokens. We used to call him Uncle Don. Don was a big drinker and smoker but he had a good side to him. For some strange reason though, my mom knew how to push his buttons and she would always get physical with him. It was like an ongoing war. They would break up and a week or two later they would be back together again.

All of their troubles always started only when they drank. My brother never did get along with him, but for some strange reason I did. I think it was because I was more of a street kid than my brother. My brother, who is eighteen months older than me, usually did very well in school. I remember times when my teacher would call my brother to her class because I was misbehaving and have a talk with him about me. My teacher also summoned my mom quite often. I think the reason why I acted out so much was because my mom would always tell me that I would never be as smart as my brother or as good as him. I think if I had a dime for all the times I heard that over my life, I'd be a millionaire.

I was constantly out playing in the schoolyard or in the streets. I loved sports. We would play stickball in the streets, drawing bases with chalk. We would compete against other kids from around the neighborhood. Sometimes we would go into the back of the fruit store where the garbage was and take all the old vegetables and fruits and have food fights in the street. We would throw eggs and fruits at each other and be covered in yolks and tomatoes and just about everything you could imagine. There usually weren't many activities to do in our neighborhood for kids so we had to make up our own fun.

I remember the two kids who lived next door to us: a brother and sister named Walter and Andrea. Just like my mother, their parents were hard, heavy drinkers. Their father used to beat his wife so bad two, maybe three, times a week, and he would also beat Walter unmercifully. He never for some reason ever hit his daughter Andrea. Mom told me their mother never really drank until she met her husband, and that she was a really nice woman, even though she drank. She was always kind to people. One day my mom told me Walter's dad had died, I thought that must have been a relief for Walter and the rest of the family. The day of the wake, Walter went up to the casket and spit on his father and just began to laugh. I felt so bad for him knowing that he had so much pain and hurt inside him and all the things that he endured in his life because of his father. I guess this was his way of getting back at him. I could relate to him because of the abuse I was going through.

CHAPTER 2

THE START OF MY
SPIRAL DOWNWARD

While attending grammar school I met up with one Charlie
Walker in the third grade. He was one of the worst guys I
would meet *and regret meeting.* Charlie had three brothers:
two younger brothers and an older one who was in the army.
Charlie was a skinny freckled face kid who liked to fight. I
guess that's why we got along so well, because I liked to fight
as well. Charlie's parents were both heavy drinkers. His dad
was a short, red-headed Irish American who drove a truck for
a living; his mom was a tough woman who reminded me of
a gun moll. She would usually have a cigarette hanging out
of her mouth, and had a mouth on her worse than a sailor's.
She knew more curse words than anyone I had ever met and
she used them a lot. They lived in a rundown house not far
from where I lived.

The very first gang in our area was called the Midnight Boys. We thought they were so cool. They had black suede jackets with a bright green clock on the back and black hands pointing to twelve o'clock; they were much older than the kids in our neighborhood. One day, Charlie and I decided to form a gang of our own, and we called ourselves the Aces. We recruited about five kids into our newly formed gang. There was Dave who we called D-Boy, Charlie's younger brother Jack who was nicknamed Freckles, Bob was nicknamed Beano, I was Ace, and of course Charlie was known as Duke. Charlie's mom would allow the boys to steal any amount of merchandise as long as it was brought back home. The local soda factory was a favorite mark. We would take our bikes to the factory in Long Island City and go to the back side where they kept the trucks which were loaded with cases of cola. One of the guys would keep a lookout while the rest of us would climb the fence. Soon twenty cases of cola were deducted from the trucks' inventory. Charlie's mom usually gave the order. We would load the cases onto our bikes and head back to his house where his mom would tell us to put it in the cellar. We stole cigarettes, candy, and gum, anything his mom or dad would tell us to steal.

His parents pretty much let them do anything they wanted most of the time, like going to school. If they didn't go, it was no big deal. There was this candy store called Franks', and the owner was a drunk. When he wanted to go out to the bar, he would ask me to watch the store. I was about eleven then. I would call Charlie and the rest of the guys and we would clean him out. We would make all kinds of sundaes and eat candy until we were sick. One day, Frank came back drunk as a skunk and fell asleep in the back room. I saw part of a twenty-dollar bill sticking out of his pants. *Wow,* I thought, *that is a huge amount of money.* About that time, Charlie came into the store and I told him Frank was passed out in the back and there was a twenty sticking out of his pocket. Charlie said, "Show me," and I did.

He reached down and took the money.

I said, "Man, you're crazy. Suppose he misses it?"

Charlie said, "He won't because he's too drunk to remember anything."

"So what are you going to do with the money?"

He said, "I'll give it to my mom. She'll know what to do with it."

So we brought it to his mom. She gave Charlie and me three dollars each and kept the rest for herself. I thought three bucks was not bad. It doesn't sound like a lot, but back then it was.

I came from a tough area. There were three older gang members, each from a different gang, and everyone feared them. They had a reputation of beating you until there was nothing left to beat: Big John, Danny, and Al. They were about seventeen. One day we were hanging out in the schoolyard when we saw Danny and John and a bunch of their gang with them. We thought they were going to have a gang fight so we started to leave at the other end of the schoolyard when Danny and John started to fight each other. So we ran over to watch. It was some brutal fight. Blood was everywhere. Everyone on each side was saying, "Kill him!" while I was shitting in my pants. I think all of the guys I was with were too. We never yelled out anything in fear of being beat up by the older gangs.

When it was over, they were both bloody. Danny beat the shit out of John. Al and his gang left, yelling threats at the others. When they were finally gone, we started to walk away when one of the older gang members said, "Where you guys think you're going?" My heart started to race, and I thought, *This is it. We're going to get our asses kicked big time.* We just stood there in fear while they came over and said, "Now squat down and grab your heels and walk and quack at the same time." And we did. They started laughing and calling us *ducks.* I guess that's what we were acting like. They made us do that for about ten minutes. Well, it's better than getting your ass kicked. When they left, we got up and took off running in fear they might return.

Just about everyone in my family smoked except for my grandmother. In fact, I think everyone in the neighborhood did. It was the thing to do then; no one knew how dangerous it was to them. Just about every kid I knew thought it was cool to be able to smoke. We used to make believe we were smoking to be cool too. They sold candy cigarettes sticks of peppermint with a red tip on the end representing the flame. We would puff on them just like real cigarettes and pretend to blow the smoke out just like the grown-ups.

My brother and I would sometimes have to attend church. When the ushers would pass around the baskets for the offering, I would stick my hand in and try to take out the money, and my brother would slap my hands and make me put it back. I thought that was pretty funny. I knew stealing was wrong, but for whatever reasons then it didn't bother me to do it. I guess I looked at it as being the cool one of the gang being told by my gang buddies that I was just as good and smart as the next guy—I was being accepted for who I was.

I used to look forward to the winters because I could make money by shoveling people's sidewalks and driveways. Sometimes I would make fifty cents for shoveling a driveway and sidewalk. It would take about two hours. The shovel I had was about three times bigger than me. It had a long wooden handle and a curved metal scoop about three feet wide at the end of it. It weighed at least eight pounds. By the time I was done shoveling, I'd be exhausted and cold, but you had to make money in those days to help out.

Everyone had to do his or her share. One thing I'll say is that we pulled together when it was necessary. Just about every kid on the block did shoveling. As a kid, my brother and I had chores to do every Saturday without fail. Our mom was very strict with us; chores had to be done or else, no questions asked. It would take us at least two to three hours of cleaning and sweeping up before we could go out and play. How I dreaded those Saturdays.

We lived in a big brownstone house with four bedrooms, a bathroom upstairs, a kitchen, and a huge dining room and living room downstairs, with a basement that was the same length and width as the house. The back of the house had a cubbyhole attached to it, a small enclosed room with a door and stairs leading to the backyard. We had some good times there, but, unfortunately to me, most were bad.

As kids, sometimes we would stand by the bus stop and when the bus came we would wait until the passengers got off, and just as the bus started to leave we would jump on the back, hanging by the tip of our fingers while our feet clung to the fender. Sure, it was dangerous, but it was fun. We would ride the bus for about a half-mile and then jump off when it came to a stop. One time we were doing it when a police car came up behind us. He sounded the siren and when the bus came to a halt we jumped off and scatted in all different directions. I knew if I got caught, I'd be in big trouble. But I was lucky. I never got caught. Playing stickball in the street was one of the big past times we loved to do. Sometimes one of the kids would saw the broom handle off so we could use it as a bat, and, usually in the middle of the game, the mom of that kid would come down and start yelling at him for ruining her broom. Of course, nobody knew where he got it from.

I remember how we would go around to the icehouse to buy ice for some of the neighbors. Back then, some people still had iceboxes to store their food in. Even the refrigerators still needed ice to help keep the food cold. We had this wagon that one of the dads in the neighborhood built. It had big baby carriage wheels on it, and to steer it he used a piece of clothesline tied to the front wheels. If we pulled left on the line, it would turn left. About five or six of us would all go to the icehouse with our wagon and get a block of ice that probably weighed a hundred pounds.

All the neighbors would chip in for it. Then they would divide the ice among each other. Just about every Saturday, it was off to the icehouse, load up the ice, and off we'd go. Two of us would jump in the wagon with the ice and the other two guys would push. Once we got going, they would jump on. There was this big hill we always went down and at the end of the hill was an avenue that crossed. We would start down this hill screaming and laughing as we sped across the avenue, praying no cars would hit us, and then make a sharp left turn. Sometimes the wagon would turn over and all of us would go flying out and the ice would slide what seemed like a hundred yards. We would have to go back and get two of the dads to get the ice back in the wagon. Of course, we would usually get into trouble for it, but it was worth it because it was fun to us.

When I was about eleven, I was walking home from a friend's house when I ran into a guy named Nick who belonged to one of the most feared gangs around: the Top Hats. Nick was known for being very skillful in knife fights, and he was only sixteen. He said to me, "Where you going, punk?"

"Home," I replied.

He said, "I don't think so. I need you to come with me to my house. I have something I need you to do for me."

I was scared, but I didn't dare let him know it because if you showed fear it was a sign of weakness and being a coward. Being in a gang myself, I knew that would mean an ass kicking from my own gang. Since I was just eleven and weighed about seventy-five pounds and was small in height for my age, and Nick being about six feet, I figured it would be best not to piss him off. "What do you need me to do?" I asked.

He looked at me with a glare that made me feel like I just said the wrong thing. He said, "Just come with me. It won't take long, and besides this will get you good points with the Top Hats."

Wow, I thought, *scoring points with them would really give me some status around the neighborhood.* So off we went to his house.

When we got there, we went down to his basement. He sat down over there and said, "I'll be right back."

A few moments passed until he finally came back and said, "Lay down on the floor."

17

"What for?" I asked.

He pulled out a switchblade. It must've had a seven-inch blade on it. "Do what I tell you."

I remember I hit that floor so fast, lying there and not knowing what was going to happen.

He knelt down and leaned over me and put the knife to my throat. I thought, *This is it. I'm dead.* I begged him not to kill me.

He said, "I'm not going to kill you, but you'd better do as I say or I will."

My heart was racing I was trembling all over.

He unzipped his jeans and forced me to perform oral sex on him. I knew if I didn't, I would be dead.

After it was over, he said, "If you say anything to anyone, you're a dead kid."

I promised him I wouldn't.

Then he said, "Get out of here."

I ran up those stairs and out of his house as fast as I could until I got about halfway down the block and started to throw up, tears running down my face. I knew I had to get it together before I got home. Deep down inside, I wanted this guy to die. I was wishing I was big enough to kick his ass, hating him with every fiber in my body, but I knew I couldn't do or say anything to anyone. So I just kept it inside of me, hoping no one ever found out.

About a month later, he sought me out again, this time performing anal sex on me.

This went on for at least three years, sometimes several times a week, sometimes more. This was the most terrible thing that ever happened to me. The pain was excruciating. I would beg him to stop, but he didn't care. I would gag and throw up. I was afraid to tell anyone. I felt if I did, people would think I was queer. In those days, people called it that instead of *gay*. If you were queer, you were considered an outcast of society. I so desperately wanted to tell someone, but there was nobody. I felt too ashamed to tell my grandparents and certainly not my mom in fear of her getting mad at me and beating me for it. I felt like it was my fault. Why? I don't know. Besides there was no one to tell me any different. There were no school counselors in those days, no counseling of any kind, so you just buried your pain inside of you. And that's exactly what I did: buried it very, very deep inside, not knowing the effect it would have upon me later on in my life.

Nick wasn't the only one I had to deal with.

CHAPTER 3

MEETING MY FATHER

One day I heard the doorbell ring. As I opened the door, there was a tall, muscular man standing there. He looked down at me and said, "Is your Mother home?"

"Who are you?"

"I'm your father."

I was about ten years old the first time I set eyes on him ... I went into the kitchen and told my mother that there was a man at the door who said he was my father. Mom let him in and they went into the kitchen and talked. A while later, my mom called me into the kitchen and said, William , this is your father." I didn't know what to do or say, so I just said hi. The next day, he came to the house and asked my mother if I could go with him to deliver some furniture. He was a moving man. I begged my mom to let me go. She said yes. As I walked down the street with him, I felt so proud. He was

21

tall with muscles and lots of tattoos on his arms. I thought, *No one could hurt me now.* Boy, was I wrong.

Later in the day, on returning, he asked me to coil the rope and hang it in the truck. I complained of being tired. He then took the rope and beat me across my legs and back. I told Mom what happened. He was gone immediately. About a year later he came back and my mom and dad were going to get back together. Mom asked me if I wanted to live with them and I said, "No, I want to stay with my grandparents." That was the last time I ever saw my father. My mom never talked about him to us after that. In fact, I don't think she ever mentioned his name again. I found out many years later that he had died at the young age of fifty-seven in Berkeley, California, from hardening of the arteries.

In 1953 I was eleven. One day, my grandfather came to me and said, "How would you like to work with me on my truck this summer?"

"Sure I would, Frankie," I said.

"I'll pay you two dollars a week."

"Sounds good to me."

He drove a truck for a company that dealt in different kinds of fruit. He would go to the docks on the waterfront, pick up these huge wooden barrels of fruit, and take them back to the warehouse. They would distribute the fruit to merchants all over the county. When I got out of school for that summer, I couldn't wait to start working with my grandfather. I felt like a real man going to work, making money.

Although he never said it to me, I think he did this because he could see I was going down the wrong path with

FROM HELL TO HIGH WATERS

the stealing and the kind of people I was hanging out with. Being from one of the toughest neighborhoods around the South Bronx, he himself was a street kid and he had street smarts like no one I have ever known. He could spot trouble a mile away.

I remember the first day he came by the house with his truck to pick me up. It was on a Monday at seven in the morning. He drove a big green truck with a picture of a chef on it with the company name under the picture. As he came into the house, I jumped into his arms and gave him a big hug and yelled, "Let's go."

"Calm down," he said. "We've got a long day ahead of us."

We both kissed my grandmother and off we went.

I was on cloud nine. Just going to work with him was awesome. He usually got up at four in the morning and would go to the warehouse to load his truck up for the day's work, and then he would come and get me. Our first stop was in Williamsburg, Brooklyn, to unload cans filled with icing. They weighed about fifty pounds each and there must've been at least sixty of them. Everything in those days was unloaded by hand. By the time we were done unloading, I was sweating like a pig, wiped out.

My grandfather looked at me and said, "Is this too much for you, son?"

"No, I can handle it."

He just smiled at me and said, "Good boy."

I could tell by the look on his face he knew it was a lot for me to handle.

That day was the hardest day of my working life; we got home about seven that night. I was sore all over my body. My grandmother asked me if I was ready for supper.

"No, I'm going to bed."

She chuckled. "All right, honey."

Thank God the next day was Saturday so I slept hours on end. My grandfather used to say to me, "Don't ever become a truck driver. There's no future in it." I worked five days a week during the summer months, about twenty hours a week. It was a lot, but just being with my grandfather was worth it.

As time went by, I continued to hang out with the wrong kind of people. The gang fights usually occurred when another gang came into our territory or if one of our members was beat up by another gang. The sexual abuse continued on the streets and the physical and mental abuse continued at home. A bunch of us went over to a friend of Charlie's where I was introduced to cigarettes. One day we went over this guy Kevin's house—he was one of Charlie's friends and was a few years older than us. He gave us each a cigarette. None of us had ever smoked before but, hey, it was the grown-up thing to do back then. I took a drag of and thought my chest was going to cave in. Little did I know it was the worst and most addicting habit I would ever encounter, but I thought it made me look older and tougher. No one knew how dangerous to your health cigarettes were. Damn, even doctors smoked in those days while they would examine you.

I was twelve then and would smoke for the next twenty-nine years.

Kevin also introduced me to some men who were in the mafia. I started running numbers for them. I would go to different stores in the neighborhood and collect money, which was to be put in a big brown paper bag, and then I would take it to the local pizza store. They knew my grandfather, but my grandfather didn't know what I was doing. I got about ten dollars for just about an hour of work, if you want to call it that. I spent the money as fast as I made it. I knew I couldn't bring it home—how would I explain where I got that much money? Most people in those days made only about a dollar an hour so me, at twelve with a ten-dollar bill, would look kind of strange.

I ran numbers for about three years. One day I went into the local bar to collect a bag of money. As I was leaving, I ran into my grandfather. He asked, "What are you doing here?"

I just stood there speechless.

"What's in the bag?" he asked.

Again I just stood silently. I was shaking all over inside. I thought he would lose his temper.

He said, "Give me the bag."

I handed the bag to him he looked inside and he just shook his head. "Come with me," he said.

We went to the pizza place where he said, "Wait out here."

He took the bag inside and I could see him grab Vinnie, the owner of the place, by the neck and push him against the wall. I couldn't hear what he said to him, but I knew it wasn't good. He came out, took me by the arm, walked me to the car, put me in, and said, "Listen, you don't need this life and your career in the mob is over."

That's all he said, and I knew I'd better listen to him.

CHAPTER 4

THE ABUSE

One day I went over to Charlie's house. I knocked on the door and his dad answered. I asked, "Is Charlie home?"

"No, he'll be back in a little while. You want to come in and wait for him?"

"Sure."

His dad seemed to have been drinking a lot. His words were kind of slurring, but that was nothing new to me; that was usual for him. "Sit down and relax. You want a soda?"

"No, thanks, Mr. Walker."

A few minutes passed. Nothing was being said, and then he got up out of his seat and came over to the couch and sat next to me. I felt really weird. He put his arm around my shoulder and said, "You're a good kid. How would you like to have some fun?"

"I think I should go now. Tell Charlie I'll see him later."

As I started to get up, he pulled me back down. "No, you need to have some fun." After all it is your tweleveth birthday tomorrow

"Get the hell away from me!" I was hoping Charlie would get home.

His dad held me down and started to molest me, grabbing me between my legs. He was too big and too heavy to get him off of me. "Please don't do this! Leave me alone!"

Shut up! You'll like it." He then sodomized me.

I was sobbing. The smell of his filthy breath made me sick.

Now what was I supposed to do? Charlie and his dad were close. He'd never believe me, and if he didn't, I knew I would take a severe beating form the gang so I couldn't take the chance. I was so sick inside when he was done. I got up and ran out of the house and rushed down the street and into an alley. I just sat there, curled up shaking, sobbing, asking myself *Why is this happening? Well, I guess I'll have to bury this along with the rest of the shit.* This was the only answer I could come up with.

I started playing hooky in the seventh grade. One time I played hooky for three weeks straight. Then one Monday morning I heard the doorbell ring, I came out of my room and leaned over the banister. I heard my mom open the door and a voice asking, "Are you Mrs. Greene?"

"Yes, I am," she answered.

"Well, I'm the truant officer and your son William hasn't been in school for three weeks."

When I heard that, I knew I was in for the beating of my life. I jumped back into my bed pretending to be sleeping. When I could hear my mother's footsteps coming up the stairs, I pulled the covers over my head. I was terrified. She threw my door to my room open, pulled the covers down, grabbed me by my hair, and dragged me out while kicking, punching, and slapping me everywhere she could. I was screaming for her to stop but don't think she heard me because she just kept whaling away on me. My grandmother had to intervene and physically restrain her. Later on, as I stood at the sink brushing my teeth and crying at the same time, my mom came up behind me and hit me in the back of the head so hard that the force sent my head forward and I gagged on my toothbrush.

As I walked down the street with the truant officer, I could hear her yelling, calling me the usual names. I think everyone in the neighborhood heard her. That was the one day I never wanted school to end, because I knew what was ahead of me when she got home from work.

When my mom came home from work that same day, she came directly to my room and took a leather belt that had metal studs on it. She pulled me out of bed by my hair. I only had on underpants and she beat me all over my body from the back of my head to my feet. I could feel the metal studs ripping into my flesh and banging against my bones. The pain was unbearable. I tried to get away, but I didn't have anywhere to go. I tried to get back into my room and shut the door. As I did, I tripped and fell to the floor. She stood over me swinging the belt, striking me in the head and back of the legs, wherever she could. I was screaming in pain at her, "Stop! Stop!"

I could hear her screaming at the top of her lungs, "You're a bum! I will kill you, you son of a bitch! You bastard! You bum! You'll never amount to anything! You'll wind up in prison!"

I honestly believed in my heart that day that if my grandmother hadn't stepped in and grabbed her, she would've beat me to death. That was just one of the many beatings I received, but also I think the worst. She threatened to send me away to a reform school.

About two weeks later, I played hooky again—this time only for a day. I thought going there would be better than being here. But she never found out about that day.

One Saturday afternoon, my Uncle Don and I were playing cards when my mom came in and said to me, "I want you to squeeze the head of a screw with a pair of pliers." I took the pliers, squeezed as hard as I could, and when I told her it wasn't working she started to hit me. She yelled, "You're useless, you bum!" She started swinging away on me as usual.

Don jumped up and told her to stop. "What the hell is wrong with you, Ann? Leave him alone."

She had been drinking as usual that Saturday, so it was nothing new to me that she acted that way. It seemed every time I turned around I was getting beaten at home or I was getting the shit kicked out of me on the streets. Of course, on the streets I guess I looked for it most of the time.

I would always pick fights with guys bigger than me and, needless to say, it was not to my advantage. I had a quick temper and would fight at the drop of a hat. If I lost, which was most of the time, I would go after the guy the next day and keep on until I either beat him or he would never want to fight me again. I got my ass kicked too many times, but I felt I had to prove to myself or to someone that I was worth something, and this was the only way I knew how. After all, violence was a big part of my bringing up.

One day in school, I was going up the staircase when my buddy hit this girl on the ass from behind. She turned around and punched me in the arm, telling me to keep my hands off her. "I didn't do it," I said. "It wasn't me."

"Yeah, right," she said.

I saw her in the schoolyard during lunch and went over to her to explain that it was my friend who did it.

"I'm sorry, I thought it was you," she said.

"That's okay, no big deal."

She had jet-black hair and dark eyes. She was beautiful. Her name was Rosa Perez, a Puerto Rican girl from the projects. She had a body on her that definitely got your attention.

I started to have lunch with her just about every day. One day I asked if she would like to go to the movies. She said, "Sure. When?"

"How about this Saturday?"

"Okay, I'll meet you in front at two o'clock."

"Cool, I'll see you then."

I felt on top of the world. I was going out with an older woman, I was thirteen and she was fourteen.

I waited for her that day. She came ten minutes late.

"I thought maybe you changed your mind," I said.

"No, I just had something to do that took longer than I thought. So you ready to go in to the show now?"

"Not really. Can we go to the ice cream parlor instead?"

"Sure." She had this sweater on that was so tight I had trouble keeping my eyes off her boobs.

After the ice cream parlor, I suggested we go back to my house to watch some television. When we got to my house, we went upstairs and sat on the sofa bed couch and watched television.

After sitting there for ten minutes or so, we started to make out. This girl had me on fire. I told her to stand up so I could pull out the sofa bed. Just as I started to do that, I heard my mom yell up to me, William " , how come it's so quiet up there?"

"We're studying!" I shouted. Damn, just when I thought I was going to lose my virginity. Of course we were both in another world. It never crossed either one of our minds that my mom might come upstairs. On Monday when I went to school, I saw Rosa and we laughed about what had happened. We both realized that if my mom hadn't called up but caught us in bed, the trouble we both would have been in if her parents found out! And knowing my mom, she would've told them. Anyway, it never did come about. After that, we more or less just became good friends. But it was an experience that I will remember for a long time to come.

One day my mother came to me and my brother, sat us both down, and then sprang on us, "You have a sister. She lives in Puerto Rico."

We both sat there in awe. She will be coming here with her husband to live with us. I looked at my mom and said, "You're not kidding are, you?"

"No, I'm not."

I found out later that my mom had been married to a Puerto Rican fellow. She had my sister, and about two years later they divorced and he took my sister back to Puerto Rico. She was raised and went to school there till she was twenty-one.

My mom went to Puerto Rico and found her but left her there because she thought she would have a better life there. I was so excited because I always wanted a sister. "When is she coming, Mom?"

"In two weeks."

My brother and I were overjoyed. I asked, "Do you have a picture of her?"

"Yes." She showed it to us. My sister was beautiful. I couldn't wait until she came.

Those two weeks seemed like a year, but finally it arrived. When I got home from school that day, I ran into the house yelling, "Did she get here yet?"

My mom said, "We're in the living room."

I ran in and there she was. I ran over and we hugged each other so tight! She was crying and I was so happy I just kept hugging her. She introduced me to her husband Jose, but I called him Joseph. He didn't speak English very well but that was okay. I told my sister I would help him with it.

My mom laughed and said, "You already ruined the king's English." That was an expression she would always use because my grammar was so bad.

During the time my sister stayed with us, things were going pretty well. One day I said to my brother-in-law, "How about letting me drive your car?"

WILLIAM THOMAS

He said, "Are you old enough?"

I thought, *He doesn't know the rules about how old you have to be to drive, otherwise he wouldn't be asking.* "Sure I am, but I have to have a licensed driver with me."

So we got into the car and I drove around the block about five times. On the fifth time, as I pulled up in front of the house, there was my sister standing on the stoop. Needless to say, she was furious. She started talking in Spanish to Jose, and, although I didn't understand a word they were saying, I knew it wasn't good. She came over to me and started screaming, "What's wrong with you? You know better. You could've gotten Jose into a lot of trouble."

"I know. I'm sorry. I won't do it again, sis."

"I'm telling Mom when she gets home."

"Please don't. She'll beat me."

"And so what? You deserve it."

Sure enough, as soon as Mom walked in the house my sister started telling her everything. Mom came at me, grabbed me by the hair, and started hitting me in the head and face, just waling on me like I was a punching bag. I knew what I did was wrong, but I sure didn't think I needed to be beaten like that.

As time went by, my sister would start telling me what to do in the house, and, when I didn't, she would tell Mom and the beatings would start. I grew to dislike her. There were times when she started to hit me when I didn't listen to her, and if I told my mom she would say I deserved it. Finally the day came when she and her husband moved out.

I was jumping with joy inside. They moved to National City, California, and I wouldn't see her for fourteen years.

When I was in the ninth grade, I made the honor role. I never thought I could do anything like that! Even my mother for the first time in my life told me I did good. I thought, *Could this be a new start in my home life? No more beatings, no more mental or emotional abuse.*

I was wishing for too much.

That same year, in 1957, my grandmother found out that she had breast cancer. I really didn't know how serious that was. She had an operation, but the cancer had spread to her lungs. My mother and grandfather had to put her in a hospice care facility Every Saturday, I would take two trains and a bus to visit her. While visiting her one day, she introduced me to one of the nuns that was taking care of her: Sister Marie Amelia. When I saw her, I thought an angel had come down from heaven. She was the most beautiful woman I ever saw, and I fell in love instantly. There was one small problem—she was about thirty-five and I was about fourteen, not to mention she was a Catholic nun.

She gave me a smile and said, "I'm pleased to meet you, William ."

I just stood there speechless. My grandmother said, "Say hello. Don't be rude.

"Oh, yeah, hi." That was all I could say.

I used to look forward to visiting my grandmother, and also I knew I would see Sister Marie. One day while visiting, I asked my grandmother, "Grammy, are you afraid to die?"

She looked at me with a smile and put her hands on my face and said, "I wouldn't change places even with you."

And then she put her arms around me as she often did and gave me a huge. I didn't want visiting hours to be over. She would always say, "Time to go now."

"But I don't want to. Let me stay."

"The hospital has rules and you have to obey them."

"Okay, but I'll be back soon."

She would give me a big kiss on the cheek and squeeze me like there was no tomorrow.

A couple of months passed and I graduated in June from junior high school 126. On graduation day, the whole family went to visit Grammy. When we got there, her bed was empty. That was usually a sign that the person died. My heart sank for a moment, and then we saw Sister Marie bring her back to the ward. What a relief it was to see her face! "Thank you, God," I whispered.

We all sat around her bed telling her about the graduation ceremony. I knew by the look on her face she wanted so much to be there. She looked at me and said, "I have something for you."

I couldn't imagine what it was. She had no money to buy anything. "Here, take this,William ."

I took the envelope and opened it and inside were fourteen dollars. "Grammy, where did you get this from?" It was a lot of money to me.

"I collected it from all the nuns here. I wanted you to have something nice for your graduation."

I reached over and hugged her as hard as I could. "Grammy, I love you so much."

"And I love you to."

We had such a great day that the hospital even let us stay an extra hour that day.

Two weeks later, on July Fourth, I was playing in the schoolyard with some friends when one of the kids from the neighborhood came and said, William your mom told me to tell you to go home right away."

I thought, *I must be in trouble.*

When I got there, the whole family was there and practically all the neighbors, and I knew when I saw them what was wrong. My grandfather said to me that Grammy had died. I just stood there not knowing what to say or do. My grandfather said, "I want you to go out and shoot off your firecrackers with your friends."

"I don't want to, Frankie."

"Go ahead. Your grandmother would want you to."

"Okay, but only because Grammy wants me to."

My mom said, "Be home no later than eight thirty."

"All right, Mom, I will."

I went back to the schoolyard and told my friends what happened; they told me how sorry they were. We shot our firecrackers off that night, and all I thought of was how much I missed my grandmother.

I got back to the house about ten minutes late that night. My mother was waiting on the stoop for me. As I walked up the steps, she said, "What did I tell you? You're late!"

I could smell the beer on her breath. She slapped me in back of the head and then pushed my head into the doorknob of the front door. I started crying, and, as I lay in my bed that night, I could hear my grandfather weeping. So I got up and went into his bed and he put his arms around me and we just lay there until I fell asleep.

The funeral was held about a week later. I never saw so many people in one place at the same time over the three days. There must've been three hundred people that came to pay their respects and tons of flowers everywhere. Everyone loved Grammy, and all were saddened by her death. Now it was my grandfather, my brother, my mom, and me.

Things never were the same. My grandfather went downhill after that. His health seemed to fail as if he had nothing to live for. After thirty-two years of marriage, I guess he felt empty without his wife. They absolutely loved each other so much. It was the most beautiful relationship I have ever seen. You could just see the love they had for each other. I used to pray that if I ever got married, I would want a relationship and the kind of love they had together. The house seemed empty and cold. I knew things would never be the same without Grammy.

I got a job that summer at the local butcher shop working about twenty-four hours six day week, for fifty cents an hour. It was hard work. Besides delivering groceries, I had to clean up the shop at the end of the day. There were these big wooden butcher blocks that the butchers would chop the meat on, and by the end of the day they had blood and fat all over them so I had this brush made with wire bristles and it was my job to scrub those blocks clean. I wasn't very tall for my age, and those blocks came up to my chest. It was hard work, but I didn't mind it so much. After all, I did get a free sandwich for lunch every Saturday. The owner, Joe Cupola, was a stocky guy who smoked like a chimney; he always had a cigarette in his mouth. He was a really good boss who never pressured me—I think maybe because he and his wife never had any kids.

Once when I was on my way to work, Charlie and the gang came by and he said, "Hey, let's go to Barney's around the corner and have some beer."

"Are you kidding? He won't let us drink."

"Yeah, well, he hired a new bartender, and I know him. He's a friend of my dad's."

"I need to get to work, guys."

"Come on, just for a little while. Then you can go."

"Okay, why not? What harm can it do anyway?"

We all headed for the bar. Normally in New York at that time you had to be eighteen to drink, but if your hand could reach the bar with the money in it there were some places that would serve you. We arrived at Barney's about three thirty. I knew I had to leave no later than four, but that didn't happen. We started to drink beer and play shuffleboard, laughing and joking and not paying any attention to the time.

The next thing I *know*, it was seven o'clock. "Damn, I have to go, Charlie. Walk home with me to my house. If my mom sees us together, she may not get mad."

What the hell was I thinking? She couldn't stand the sight of Charlie.

When we got to my house, we very quietly opened the door and went into the kitchen. It was real quiet in the house. "Charlie, my mom must be asleep."

And then we heard the footsteps coming down the stairs. It felt like the whole house started to rumble. The kitchen door flew open and there she was. "You son of a bitch!"

Charlie turned white and ran past her like lighting, and out the door he went. She picked up a kitchen chair and threw it at me. I ducked, but it landed on my back. I ran around the kitchen table and managed to make it up the stairs to my room and barricade my door. My grandfather wasn't home. I could hear her screaming as she came up the stairs and tried to get in, but thankfully she couldn't.

The next day, to my surprise, nothing was said to me. No beating either. I found out later that my grandfather had spoken to her about what happened. I guess whatever he said to her worked.

In September 1957 I started my first year of high school. I was so excited because I knew there were all kinds of different activities we didn't have in junior high. One day, as I was sitting in English class, this girl walked in. She came to collect the morning's attendance book, and she sometimes worked in the school office. The first time I saw her as she entered the classroom I thought she was an angel. She had long blond hair, hazel eye, and was incredibly beautiful. *I will have to get to know her.* One day after class, I saw her talking with some people in the hallway so I just waited until she was done. I started to walk in her direction, and, as I looked at her, she gave me a big smile and said hi. I said hi and told her, "You're the girl who comes into my English class every morning. I'm William ."

"I'm Pamela , nice to meet you William ."

"Same here."

We talked for a while and then the bell rang for the next class to start.

"I have to go. Nice talking with you,William ."

"See you tomorrow, Pamela."

"Okay."

I could hardly wait for that day to come. After school that day, I went to work at the butcher shop. That evening I decided to quit the gang, I went over to Charlie's house and told him that I was quitting. "I don't think so," he said.

"Yeah, I do."

He said, "Fine."

But something was wrong. I knew I couldn't just walk away from them. I left that night and went to a friend's house. His name was Tony Giovanni and we had been good friends for a long time, although he belonged to another gang. They weren't rivals of our gang. I told him what I did.

He said, "If anything happens to you, I'll make sure we get them."

"Thanks, Tony. I owe you."

On my way home from Tony's house, I got jumped by Charlie and the rest of gang. They beat me up pretty bad. I fought as hard as I could, but I was taking on seven or eight guys; it was a no-win situation for me.

After it was over, I managed to get back to Tony's house. He took me down to the basement and cleaned me up. He said, "Well it didn't take them long to get you."

I looked at him through my bloody face and smiled. "I guess not."

"Don't worry, you'll get even."

That night when I got home, my mom was asleep and I knew that she would be gone early the next morning so I wouldn't have to explain what happened. My grandfather came into my room, took one look at me, and said, "You quit the gang, didn't you?"

"How did you know?"

"Because the last time *I* looked like you do now is when I did the same thing."

"I smiled. "Yeah, you guessed it."

He came over and sat down beside me. "Listen to me. Over my life time I got mixed up with some of the most notorious people in the country, and I'm telling you now it's time to change your ways or there will come a day when it will be too late."

I knew deep inside he was right. I looked at him and said, "Thank you, Frankie."

The next day I got up for school and, as I was washing, my brother came in and said, "What the hell happened to you?"

"I fell."

"Sure you did."

I knew I would see Pamela so when she came into my class to collect the attendance records I put my head down so she wouldn't see my face. When class was over, I went out the back door of the classroom and hurried down the hall to get to my next class, hoping I wouldn't run into her. But as my luck would have it, I heard her voice. " William , wait a minute." I stopped and turned around as she asked, "What happened to you?"

"I got into a fight."

"Are you okay?"

"Yeah, I'm fine. Say, would you like to go to the movies Friday night?"

"Yes, I would, William ."

I thought, *You might say no when you saw my face messed up like this.* I didn't know what else to say. I do know that I was glad she liked me. "I'll pick you up around five."

"That sounds good. See you then."

That whole week seemed to just drag. I couldn't wait until I saw her again. Finally, Friday was here/ I went over to pick her up. She lived in an apartment house on the top floor and there was no elevator so I climbed up ten flights of stairs. By the time I got to the top, I felt like I needed resuscitation. *Damn, why can't she live on the first floor?*

After the movie, we took a walk. "Hey, let's stop here for a minute," I said. I took her by the hand and walked over to a car that was parked and lifted her so she could sit on the fender. I stood there for a minute and looked at her and asked, "Can I kiss you?"

She shied away with her head down. "I'd like that."

I knew that this was my first real love in life. She had this incredible way about her, something soft and gentle, and kind of shy in her own way.

The next day I went to the pool with some friends and ran into Tony. "What's up, William ?"

"Nothing much. Those guys who jumped you a few nights ago, we took care of them. We did a number on them. They won't forget for a long time."

"Thanks, Tony. I owe you."

"Nah, that's okay. Forget about it."

"Cool, man, thanks again."

"Hey, William, you want to join us? We could always use someone. Become one of the Park Side Gents." That was the name of Tony's gang. They were, after all, one of the toughest gangs around, but then I remembered what my grandfather said to me. Obviously I never listened. One thing for sure: when you're in a gang, you have no friends because real friends would never want to get you in trouble or see you beat up. And if Pamela ever found out, that would be the end of us.

"I think I'll pass on this one."

"Okay, but if you ever need anything, we're here for you."

"Cool, thanks, Tony."

Two years passed. I managed to stay out of trouble and didn't see much of the gang I used to run with. My brother got drafted into the army, and my grandfather moved in with his brother in Rockaway. Now it was just me and my mom in that big house. She still drank heavily on the weekends, mostly with my Aunt Jennie, a neighbor who knew our family for years. She really wasn't our aunt, but we used to call her that. She was a very kind woman who would do anything for anyone.

The one thing I remember the most about Aunt Jennie is that she's the only lady I knew who could eat a whole chocolate cake. In fact, she always ate sweets more than regular food. I'm surprised she didn't have diabetes. I know the local bakery loved her. She smoke like a chimney, one after another. I even remember the cigarettes she smoked: Regents. Her husband James was a quiet guy who worked as a janitor for a large computer company. They had two kids: Rose and Kyle. Rose and I would constantly get into fistfights. She was the tomboy of the block. One Easter, a bunch of us kids went to Central Park and Rose and I were messing around and fell into a shallow pond. We came home with mud all over us, my new Easter suit and her new dress covered in mud. Our parents had a fit. I only suffered a spanking that day.

CHAPTER 5

ENTERING THE ADULT WORLD

My brother got shipped to Fort Dix, New Jersey, for his basic training. About every other week, my mom and I would go down to visit him. He looked really cool in his uniform. After his basic training, he was shipped to San Antonio, Texas, where he studied to be a corpsman. That's a male nurse. Later on, he got shipped overseas to Frankfurt, Germany, where he spent the rest of his enlistment. When I reached seventeen I asked my mother to sign me out of school.

I quit school to help with the bills and rent. I managed to get a job with Pan American World Airways as a courier, making fifty dollars a week. That was a lot of money in 1959. Mom continued to work at the factory and drink on the weekends, but the beatings had ceased. I guess she decided I was too old to beat anymore, but the mental abuse continued.

I decided that the best thing to do was to get out, so I went to my mother and asked her to sign me into the United States Naval Reserve—since I was under age I needed her consent. At first, she was reluctant, but she finally gave in. I had to be in at least a year before I could go on active duty.

I continued to work for Pan Am where I hung out with older guys. Most of them were in their late twenties. I met a guy named Johnny who had been with the company since he graduated high school. He was twenty-eight. Johnny and I became pretty close friends. Every other Friday on payday we would go out to a big Italian dinner and then go drinking at the Beef and the Bird, a club on Steinway Street, and drink and party until closing, which was about four in the morning. That was just the start of my drinking days. The next morning my head would feel like a train ran over it. I thought it was cool to party like this; little did I know what effect it would have on me down the road, but remember that was a way of life back then. After all, I was hanging out with the adults, and besides, all I ever knew was abuse and drinking.

On Christmas Eve, we got off from work early and all of us guys went down to Smugglers Cove, a bar that most of the people in the company usually went to on a Friday after work. I was sitting with some of the guys when this red- headed woman came up to me and said, "You want to dance?" She had this green dress on that clung to every part of her body.

"You bet I would." So I got on the dance floor with her. She just rubbed against me while dancing, and I could feel my knees start to buckle. I found out later she was thirty-seven, and here I was seventeen. She put her arms around my neck and kissed me. Oh, my God! I never been kissed like that before! I was trembling everywhere.

"Would you like to take me home?" she asked.

"Oh, yes."

I went over to the guys and asked them for some money for a taxi. One said, "No, we're sorry, we can't do that. You might get into trouble."

"Good. Let me just give me some money."

But to no avail. She walked out of the bar and I never saw her again. Damn, I was mad. The next day I found out that the guys had set the whole thing up as a joke. "You guys suck!" I shouted. They were laughing so hard, and then I started laughing.

The old neighborhood had changed. A lot of the people on the block had moved away or died either from alcohol or just old age. I was starting to party more; I stopped seeing Pamela for the most part. I was too busy having what I thought was a good time.

That year went by pretty fast. The next thing I knew, it was time for me to go to the naval training camp at the Great Lakes in Chicago, Illinois. The guys at work threw me a big party down at Smugglers Cove. There must've been at least forty people there from work. It lasted way into the early morning hours. I'm glad I didn't have to report to the local naval center that morning to pick up my orders for boot camp. I would've have been too hung over.

Two days later, I got up early, packed my suitcase, and got ready to leave for the Great Lakes. My mom was in the kitchen having coffee. I went and said good-bye. I kind of felt bad for her. My brother was still in Germany in the army, and here I was leaving home as well. I must admit, though, that I was glad to get out of there. That was one of the very few times I can remember my mom hugging me. She said, "Take care of you."

"I will."

That was about it. No tears. Just plain and simple.

By the end of the day, I had arrived at boot camp. It was freezing and windy, which made it worse. It was in the middle of January. New York was cold, but not this bad. I was processed along with about a hundred other guys and then assigned to C barracks, Company A-1. After I got all my gear unpacked, it was off to the barbershop where I would lose all my hair. We had to get up at four thirty every morning. The company leader would come in every morning and make the loudest noise I think I ever heard. He would take a Coke bottle and rattle it inside a garbage can. We thought the roof was caving in. That's one noise you don't want to hear at four thirty.

Then we would have to line up outside the barracks and stay there until everyone was out and in line. There were always some stragglers making the rest of us stand there that much longer. Then it was off to the chow hall for breakfast.

My drinking had subsided while I was at boot camp since you had to be twenty-one to drink. My training at the Great Lakes Naval training center lasted three months, and then I was shipped to the Brooklyn Navy Yard in New York where I would spend about a month. There was an aircraft carrier there called the USS Franklin D. Roosevelt, which was having an overhaul done to her. The navy always refers to the ships as women. When I laid my eyes on her, I knew I wanted to be a part of her crew, so I asked the chief petty officer that was in charge of transfers how I could get on her. He said, "You have to put in a request form and have it approved by the commanding officer of the base." I did just that, and about two weeks later my request came through approved. I was so excited! I was going to travel the world! I felt like the luckiest kid alive.

As I walked up the gangplank to board Rosie—that was the crew's name for her—I turned and saluted the flag at the back of the ship. And then I saluted the officer of the deck and requested permission to come aboard. As I walked into the hangar bay, where they kept the aircraft, I noticed it was huge. I felt like a tourist in New York looking up at the tall buildings.

I was assigned to the hangar bay, division A. Its job was to take care of the upkeep of the hangar bays, all three of them, and to park the aircraft in the order of which planes would be called to the flight deck. Each bay must've been hundred and fifty feet long, seventy feet wide, and thirty feet high. Rosie must've carried about sixty planes or so. She was a little more than three football fields long and her flight deck was about six stories high above the water.

After about three months in the navy yard, we were finally leaving and heading to the Naval Air Station in Mayport, Florida. That's where our homeport was while in the United States. We would stay there for about a month and then head to Cuba to the navy base Guantanamo Bay, affectionately known to the military as Gitmo.

My drinking soon started up again while I was in Florida. That's what a lot of the sailors did when we went on liberty—

drinking and getting into barroom brawls. That went on throughout most of my enlistment. I did get to travel a lot. I went overseas to Italy, France, Greece, Spain, and Gibraltar. I remember how the people in some of those countries were so poor. Those little children seven or eight years old would come up to us and ask us, "Do you want to come home and make love to my mom?" Or sometimes it would be their sister. Some of the guys did, but I just couldn't see the sense in that. It was like taking advantage of their unfortunate situation, so I just gave them some money instead to buy food.

Life was tough over there. In nineteen sixty They were still built up from the war twenty years later. I saw a portion of the devastation that war can leave behind: ruins, poverty, sickness, and a desperation to survive How sad it was to me. It did make me think of how blessed I was to have been born here in the United States. The one thing I learned, if nothing else, is that I did get to see how other people live and their cultures, even though some of it was sad. I think it matured me more in life as far as being more appreciative.

After six months of touring the Mediterranean Sea, we returned home to Mayport, Florida, at last back in the United States. The first thing I did was put in for a thirty-day furlough to go home. It was around Christmastime and I was anxious to spend the holidays in New York. My mom had moved into a two-bedroom apartment while I was away. The house was too big, and most of the people in the neighborhood had moved; everything was so different. New people came into the neighborhood so it seemed empty.

I didn't have enough money to take a bus or fly. I wanted to bring my mom a present, but all I could afford was a small picture of my ship. I thought she would like to have that so she could show her friends the ship I was serving on. It took me three days to get home. I think I must've ridden in twenty different cars; I met some strange characters while hitchhiking. There was this one guy who claimed he was a bodyguard for Howard Hughes, but he claimed he only worked part-time for him. When I heard that, I laughed so hard inside. I figured if I laughed out loud, he'd flip out. I just never heard of a part-time bodyguard. Then there was this woman who I don't think ever shut up. She just went on and on for at least a hundred miles. She never really made any sense. Maybe she just needed someone to listen to her. Unfortunately it was my ears that took the beating.

I arrived home in the morning. I knocked on the door and my mother's boyfriend Don, who was now my stepdad, answered. "Welcome home,William , nice to see you." He shook my hand.

"Nice to see you to Don."

My mom came out of the bedroom with her greeting, "Don't you know it's two in the morning?"

I guess that wasn't bad since I hadn't seen her for eight months. I walked over and gave her a hug. "I'm going to hit the hay. We can talk in the morning, if that's okay, Mom."

"Sure, good night. See you later."

The next morning I got up about eleven and went into the kitchen. Don was sitting there with my mom having coffee morning. Mom asked, "Would you like some coffee?"

"No thanks, Mom. I'll just grab some oatmeal."

My brother was still sleeping so I went in and woke him up. "Hey, what's up?" I said. "Get out of bed, you bum."

"Hey, how are you?" He shook my hand and we sat and talked about some of the places I had traveled.

My brother and I were never really close. I think it was because of how my mom kept telling me how much smarter he was and how I would never be as good his him. The next day was Christmas Eve. Things sure changed over the years! My mom hardly had any decorations up and just a small artificial table tree. It seemed like it was just another day; she had no Christmas spirit. On Christmas morning, I went and saw some friends. Later that afternoon I returned home. As we were ready to sit and have dinner, I gave my mom the present I had bought her. She opened it up and when she saw it was a picture of the ship I was on, she said, "You call this a present? I can't believe you. How dare you give me something like this!"

"But Mom, I thought you would like it. I couldn't afford anything else."

She looked at me with a glare. "You ought to be ashamed of yourself."

Needless to say, I felt like shit. I didn't get it. Why was she so disappointed? Even when I did the best I could, it was not good enough. I should've been used to it by now, but somehow you never get used to mental abuse or any other kind. It wasn't a very merry Christmas that year. I decided this was not where I wanted to be so I packed up my sea bag the next day and headed back to Florida.

I took a train into the city where I caught a bus to Florida. I only had forty-two dollars on me, and that's exactly how much the fair was. There was nothing here for me just misery so I figured, *What the hell. I might as well go back.* It was going to take eighteen hours and that meant no food since I was broke.

I had a seat next to this woman and her baby. We started talking, and after about an hour she asked me a few times to hold the baby while she used the restroom. I had no problem with that. What I had a problem with was her saying to me, "You sure would make a good dad." That's all I needed—a baby and a wife at nineteen years old! I knew then it was time to change seats, but unfortunately there weren't any. So I just had to sit there and listen to what a great dad I could be. Besides listening to my stomach growl of hunger and her, I kept thinking, *Wake up. It's just a dream.* That was the longest trip I think I had ever taken. Instead of hours, it seemed like weeks. I was so thankful when we finally pulled into the bus terminal in Florida. I knew right then and there that there was a God.

I immediately got off the bus and hitchhiked a ride back to the ship where I borrowed some money from one of my friends and went over to the canteen and filled my face with food. Then I went back to ship and settled in for a long night's sleep.

About nine months later, I got discharged from the navy. I returned home and the very first thing I did was go and see Pamela . I never realized how much she really meant to me; it took me years to finally realize it. When I saw her, we hugged each other and kissed. I said to her, "Let's take a walk." Just like we always did, since I still didn't have a car. We stopped by a parked car. I picked her up and sat her on the fender and asked her if she would be my wife. She put her head down. "What's wrong?"

She looked up at me. "I want to,William , but you're just too wild."

Inside, I knew she was right. "But I'll change."

"No you won't."

"I swear I will."

"No,William , I'm sorry."

I looked at her and I knew I had really messed up. I gave her a kiss. "Come on, I'll take you home."

I took three weeks off before I went back to work, just having one big party. A couple of months later I met a girl named Ruth who worked for the same company as I did. We started dating and it got pretty serious. She to liked to drink and party. It was in January when I got the news from my boss that I was getting laid off. When I got home that evening I told my mom that I had lost my job. She told me I had to leave.

I packed whatever little items I had and headed out. I called some friends but they didn't seem to have any room, so they said. I wound up sleeping in hallways on cold marble floors of different apartment buildings and underneath staircases. Unfortunately for me, it was winter and damn cold. After about a month of sleeping around in the streets, I finally told my girlfriend what had happened. Her parents let me stay in the basement of their house until I got a job, which I thought was really nice.

One night when I was sleeping in the basement, I heard someone coming down the stairs. I got up and asked, "Who's there?" The light went on and my girlfriend's brother was holding a twelve-gauge double-barrel shotgun in my face. I just about shit my pants. He thought I was a burglar. Needless to say, I'm glad I wasn't. I stayed there for two weeks, and then I found a place in a boarding house. I lived in one room. I had to share the bathroom, shower, and refrigerator with seven other people. The house was rundown and not in the best part of town, but I had to do what I could afford. I continued to see my girlfriend Ruth, but that only lasted for a few weeks more. I found out that she had been cheating on me for almost a year. After that happened, I thought, *What's wrong with me?* My life just seemed to be a pile of shit: the abuse, the drugs, and choosing the wrong people to hang out with. *I'm just a waste*, I thought. *Is this what my life is going to be like?* I was trying inside to hold on. I wanted to be liked and accepted, but most of all to be loved.

I was living in garbage and being treated like I was a piece of trash. I asked myself what I was doing to make people, even my own parents, treat me like this. I was tearing at my soul, aching in my heart trying to find the answer. *How long do I have to go on like this? When will I find peace within me?*

Being alone was the worst thing I ever experienced. I had no real friends.

CHAPTER 6

MEETING MY FUTURE WIFE

In 1963, I got a job working for an air conditioning company in Maspeth, New York, as offset press operator. I would come home after work and just sit in my one-room apartment with no one to talk to. It was one of the worst parts of my life—nothing to do, just loneliness.

Just when I thought all was lost, I went to work one morning and I saw this girl in the next office. She was kneeling down at the file cabinet, and I thought, *She is so good looking, and what great legs she has!* I called my friend Robert over and said, "You see that girl there? I am going to marry her."

"You don't even know her."

"You're right, I don't know her, but I will."

I asked her girlfriend Camille what her name was. She responded, "Her name is Frances."

"I sure would like to take her out."

"Don't waste your time. She's engaged and is getting married in three months."

I thought, *That gives me until June to steal her from her boyfriend.*

As the days went by, I got to know Frances and we became friends. We started having lunch together about twice a week; we hit it off from the start. She had this shy way about her like a little girl. Any time I would look into her eyes and not say anything, she would turn red like an apple and giggle. "Stop it," she would say.

"Why? Don't you like the way I look at you?"

"Yeah, I do."

The lunches turned into five days a week. We seemed to like each other a lot, but I knew she would never tell me how much she liked me because of her engagement. But it didn't matter because I could see that she did. There would be times that she would come to work very sad. "What's wrong?" I would ask her.

"It's my boyfriend."

He would get physical with her. I said, "So why don't you break up with him and go out with me?"

"I can't William . My mom would be furious. I'm supposed to get married in a month and a half."

I wanted to kick this guy's ass so bad for what he was doing to her, but I knew I couldn't do that. It would cause too many problems for her. What a punk he was hitting on a woman.

About a week later the company was having a party. I didn't really want to go since I had no one to take, but I figured, *What the hell. I might as well. Maybe I'll some fun.* When I arrived at the party, I saw Frances. I went over and asked her if she was with her boyfriend.

"No, he's not with me."

"That's great. So it's just me and you."

She smiled. "Stop it, you're so bad."

"Who, me? Never." I had a sly grin on my face. "Would you like to dance?"

"Sure, I would."

What an incredible dancer she was! Smooth on her feet like a swan flowing through the water.

Later on that evening, one of the guys who worked in Frances's office came over to me, James, an arrogant, self-centered, egotistical ass who thought he was God's gift to women. In other words, he was a real jerk–off. He said, "You need to stop dancing with Frances. My friend Glen likes her."

"Really? I don't think so." I said.

She looked at him with a glare in her eyes like she wanted to sock him. "You're an idiot, Jim. Let's go,William ."

So we left the party and got into her car and drove up to this church on a hill where I used to go as a kid. We sat on the steps and talked for a while, and then I leaned over and kissed her. I thought she might pull away, but she didn't. We had a good time that evening. It was like we were meant to be together forever. I fell for her like a ton of bricks and I was hoping she felt the same way, but I didn't dare ask in fear of rejection. I knew time was running out—soon she would be getting married. All I could do now was pray that by some miracle she wouldn't walk down that aisle in June.

Then one day at work, Camille a friend of Frances, came and told me that Frances had broken her engagement."

I said, "You're kidding me?"

"No, she really did. Go ahead, get in there, and ask her out."

I just about tripped over my own feet rushing into her office. I could see she had been crying. I played it like I didn't know what was going on. "What's wrong?"

"I just broke up with my boyfriend."

"I'm so sorry." Like I wasn't happy my miracle had come true! Hallelujah! "Why don't we go out tonight?"

"I don't feel like doing anything right now."

"Come on, do you really think he's going to sit home and worry about how you feel?"

I managed to persuade her to go out with me that evening. I picked her up down the street from her house because she didn't want her family to know that she was going out with someone. Besides, her ex-boyfriend's aunt owned the house they lived in and she lived on the lower floor.

We went bowling that night over in Jamaica, a few blocks from my old neighborhood. Things were going pretty well when her ex showed up with his brother. He came over to us and said to Frances he needed to talk to her. She said, "I have nothing to say to you. Now leave us alone."

He gave me a look and I just stood there and looked back, waiting for him to make his move, but he didn't. He turned and left. I pretended like everything was okay, but I was hoping he would start with me.

From that day forward, she and I saw each other almost every day. We were inseparable; we went everywhere together. Once I had taken her to Forrest Park, a local lovers lane. When we pulled in, there must have been at least a hundred cars or more. We sat there listening to the music on the radio. She lay down in my arms and we just sat there not saying a word as we looked into each other's eyes. Suddenly I heard this bang on the window. The windows were all fogged up so you couldn't see in. I rolled down the window and there was a police officer and he said we needed to leave the park. He said that the park was closing and we had been parked here for three hours. I looked out the window and, sure enough, we were the only ones left. We never heard a car leave. We were in our own world.

That was the first time I sat with a girl and looked at her that long without at least trying to cop a feel.

She had three brothers and one sister, a mom from Ireland and a dad from Quebec, Canada. Her dad owned a butcher shop where her twin brother, Brad, and her oldest brother, Harold, worked. Her youngest brother, Erwin, worked in a bakery around the corner from the shop. Her sister, Ellen, lived out on the island in Bayshore with her husband, Allan. They had two small children—Eve and Leigh—and later had a boy named Bob. Frances's mom didn't want to meet me so I would always have to pick her up down the street from her house. This went on for about five months. I asked Frances why she didn't want to meet me or why I couldn't pick her up at the house. She said it was because of her ex-fiancé's aunt who owned the house and she felt embarrassed that the aunt would see me and start asking her questions. This went on for about five or six months. Then one day Frances called and told me that her mom wanted me to come to dinner on Sunday

"Are you sure it's okay?" I asked.

"Yes, my whole family will be here."

"Your whole family? I don't know, hon, if I can handle this."

"You'll be fine. Just come. I'll see you on Sunday."

I arrived at her house about one in the afternoon. I was real nervous about meeting her family, but I was also glad because that meant maybe I wouldn't have to pick her up down the street anymore. I was hoping they would like me. Things went pretty well. Her brothers and sister were really cool. There were three brothers and one sister. Her mom was born in Dublin, Ireland, and a had a thick Irish brogue. It took some getting used to to understand her, but you wouldn't dare tell her that because she would definitely read you the riot act. Her dad was kind of a quiet man. He really didn't say too much to me so I wasn't really sure what he thought of me.

After about a year of dating Frances, I finally decided it was the right time to pop the question. So one Saturday I went over to her house to pick her up. When I got there, her mom said she was up in her room. I asked, "Can I go up and see her?"

"Sure."

I went upstairs. "Hi, honey. I need to talk to you."

"About what?"

I sat on her bed. "Come over here and sit on my lap."

She sat down and put her arms around my neck. I looked into her eyes and without hesitation I asked her, "Would you marry me?"

"Are you serious?"

"Yes, I am."

She started to cry and then I said, "I'm just kidding."

She jumped off my lap and said, "You suck!"

I laughed. I pulled her back down and said, "Of course I mean it."

"Don't do that to me. That was mean."

"So will you?"

"Yes, of course, I will."

I was the happiest guy in the world. I was so crazy about her; everyone would always say what a great couple we made. We got engaged in September 1964 and one year later we would get married on her birthday: September 12, 1965.

In January 1965, nine months before the wedding, we got some bad news that her mom had a fatal liver disease. In April, the doctor told her she needed to go into the hospital, but she refused to do it. Everyone in the family was trying to talk sense into her, so one day she asked me if I would talk with her. "Mom," as I would always call her, "you need to go or else you will get sicker."

She looked at me and said, "If I go into the hospital, I know that I will not be coming back."

I told her, "Yes, you will. I promise you. For the life of me, until this day, I still don't know why she listened to me, but she went. Her condition was getting worse.

Frances and I went to visit her. It was like she was totally at peace. She had a glow to her like an angel from heaven was with her. I went over to her and she said, " William , I want you to have my crucifix, and I'll dance with you at your wedding."

"Yes, you will. I'm counting on it." And with that, I turned to Frances and we hugged each other and she passed away. She had a look on her face of peace and a glow as if an angel came down and took her to God. That was a very sad day for Frances and her family.

On September 12, 1965, we were married at Saint James Episcopal Church in Elmhurst, New York. The reception was held in Brooklyn at Dante's. We had set a place for her mom at the table as if she was there, and we believed she was.

We had a great wedding. About 175 people showed up. The minster who married us was about three shades to the east that day, just another way of saying he had one too many to drink. He asked me if I would take Frances to be my lawful wedded husband. Everyone in the church laughed. He finally got it straight and we were pronounced man and wife.

Ten years later, the church burnt down, and a year after that the reception hall burnt as well. I never knew what to make of that. Maybe it was an omen.

We went to Bermuda for our honeymoon; since my grandmother was born and raised there, I had a lot of relatives whom I had never met. My mom told me that there were a lot of aunts, uncles, and cousins that live there, and when we get there to look them up. It turned out that there were about a hundred relatives and we didn't meet them all. They treated us like they knew us all of their lives; they just couldn't do enough for us.

The ten days we were there were the best times in my life. When we got back to the states, we moved to Sunnyside in Queens. We had a nice apartment in a two-family home on the top floor: two bedrooms, one bath, the rooms were big, and the rent was 135 dollars a month. That was a lot of money to us back then.

I started a new job delivering laundry to homes. It was okay, but I wasn't crazy about it. In fact, I had twenty-five jobs in twenty-four months. If I didn't like a job or if the boss gave me a hard time, I would just quit. I would never give them the satisfaction of firing me. One job I had you weren't allowed to talk to your coworkers during working hours so I quit. That job lasted one day. Not the smartest thing to do, but I was one of those guys with an attitude who wouldn't take nothing from no one. Jobs were plentiful back then. You could quit a job in the morning and have one by that afternoon, not like today where jobs are scarce.

I always worked. we were doing fine, but I knew I had to get a steady job with a future. I'm glad we didn't have any children then or else it would have been really tough.

In January I got a job driving over the road with Greyhound Bus Line. It paid great. The problem was I was always on the road going to Montreal, Canada, mostly for the world exposition. I hardly got to see my wife. It was taking a real toll on me and on her. It was like we were becoming strangers never having time together, so I decided to leave the bus company and look for a job that would allow me to be home more often. A friend of mine told me to try some of the airlines—he had heard they were hiring. So I applied for a job with United Airlines in October of that year. A month later I was hired on with them, and left the bus company; at last a normal job with normal hours and time home with my wife.

We moved closer to the airport and lived in a one-bedroom apartment in Corona. The rent was a lot cheaper—only ninety dollars a month That was better than what we were paying even though it was a smaller place. Most of the people were Italian and everyone seemed to be friendly. Frances worked as a bookkeeper for a firm in Elmhurst just down from her father's butcher shop. I hired on at the airlines on Thanksgiving Day, working as a ramp serviceman. I loaded and unloaded passenger planes and freighter planes. I was making two dollars and ninety-seven cents an hour. Not a lot of money, but it was a fair wage in 1967. I didn't much care for working holidays, but it was extra money and that always helped.

I worked at Idlewild Airport, which was later renamed John F. Kennedy International Airport in his memory. I became close friends with one of the guys I worked with. Elwood and his wife Carol had four daughters. We spent most of our days off with them hanging out and going on vacation. They were good people. Elwood's brother-in-law Pete lived next door to him and Elwood would tell me that everything he bought Pete would have to buy. So one day I suggested that he rent something, and then Pete would buy it and that might end it. Elwood came to work one day and told me he rented a brand-new Ford Thunderbird for a week, and by the end of the week Pete had purchased one himself. When Pete asked him, "What happened? Where's your car?" Elwood replied, "Oh, that was a rental just for the week. Pete just stood there with his mouth opened and Elwood walked away.

I laughed so hard. I said, "You're kidding! You didn't really do that."

"Yeah, I did."

"Damn, Elwood , I just meant to rent something small, not a new car."

He laughed and said, "I bet he won't be copying me anymore." And believe it or not, he didn't. He couldn't. He didn't have enough money to, not with a car payment.

I worked at Idlewild for about a year and then I transferred to LaGuardia Airport. Elwood and I still remained friends even though I was working at a different airport. I was working the 1:00 p.m. to 9:30 p.m. shift. I loved those hours. I could sleep late in the morning, no alarm clock going off, and still be able to go out with Frances in the evenings or just stay home. It was nice being able to be with her instead of seeing her maybe two or three times a month like when I worked for the bus company. Everything was going well.

In January 1969, we took a trip to California to see my sister who I hadn't seen for ten years. She had three children by now, and I was looking forward to the visit. When we arrived in California, we stayed at my sister's house for the short weekend we spent there. I fell in love with California.

The weather was awesome even in the winter, compared to New York. When we got home I told Frances I wanted to move there. I could put in for a transfer and continue to work for the airlines there.

She said, "I don't know. Our families are all here."

"I know they are, but with the free passes I get we can come back at least six times a year, and in another three years I'll have unlimited passes. I could see she still wasn't sure. "Please, please," I begged her. "I promise I'll stop biting my nails." That was a habit I had that she wanted me to break.

"You will? Are you sure? You promise?"

"Yes, I will." My fingers were crossed behind my back.

"Okay, let's do it."

"You're the best, honey."

The next day, I went to work and put in for a transfer to Los Angeles, California. I figured it would take about two months to hear anything. Well, to my surprise, my transfer came through a week later and I had to be in California in two weeks. We sold everything we owned except for our clothes and a few pots, pans, and dishes.

We stayed with my sister who lived in National City until we could find a place of our own. I reported to work a couple of days later on the midnight shift. They assigned me to the airfreight facility, which was a lot different compared to working on the ramp loading passenger planes. About three weeks later we found a really nice apartment just across the street from Metro-Goldwyn-Mayer Studios, not far from where my sister lived. It was a one-bedroom furnished apartment for 120 dollars a month. The manger was Mr.

Simmons, an elderly gentleman who was about to retire. A couple that lived there became the new mangers, Renee and Phil, about a month later when Mr. Simmons retired. They were very nice people; Phil also worked as a painter besides managing. Renee had two grown children from a previous marriage. She handled the rentals and Phil did the maintenance for the apartments.

We became close friends with them over the next few months; Phil drank a lot, which was not good for me to be around at the time. What I never knew was that I had an addictive personality and, slowly but surely, I started drinking again. First I thought, *Well, I just won't drink as much as I used to.* But it eventually took hold of me once again. From there I started going out after work with the guys drinking and then, like a jerk, driving my car home. We met our neighbors who later on moved in next door to us, Mike and Sharon. He was from South Dakota and Sharon was from California. Mike and I would go out to the bar and usually come home drunk. We met other people at the apartments. It was like a big party. The wives of the guys drank, but not like the guys did. There was no doubt the situation was out of control. What I didn't know is that I was an alcoholic. My life was out of control and I thought I was in control. That's how sick you get with false thoughts.

A few months later, in June, Frances went to the doctors for a checkup and the next day the doctor called the house. I answered the phone and he told me that we were going to have a baby! I had been asleep and when I heard the news I don't think it registered because I said, "Okay, thanks, Doc," and hung up. I went back to sleep. When Frances got home from work that evening, she came in and woke me up. As I looked up at her with glassy eyes, I told her, "You're pregnant."

"What?"

Then it finally hit me and I jumped up out of bed and hugged her and yelled, "That's right! The doctor called. We're going to have a baby!"

We were so happy.

"I hope it's a boy," I said.

"You do? And suppose it's a girl?"

"But I really want a boy."

She laughed. "It doesn't matter as long as the baby's healthy, and you're right honey, that's all that counts. So what should we name him?"

"Why don't we wait and find out if it's a boy or girl first."

"I suppose you're right."

We called our folks back home to give them the good news. I felt so proud of my wife. She was going to have a baby.

I started saving for a crib so our child could have a nice place to sleep. I felt like a kid myself. I was busting inside. I was hoping I could be a good father, not like mine who took off but more like my grandfather who was strict but kind. I was determined that our child would not grow up in an abusive environment, and definitely not be in a gang.

I was always telling Frances, "Don't do this" or "Don't do that. You're pregnant. I don't want you to hurt yourself."

She would look at me with a smile. "Exactly. I'm pregnant, not an invalid. I can do things for myself."

I suppose I was being overprotective, but I wanted to make sure she and the baby would be okay.

I remember the day we went for our first ultrasound so we would actually see the baby. We arrived at the doctor's office and they took us into where they would do the ultrasound. As they prepared Frances for the examination, I grew more excited. Finally, the nurse came in and we got to see our very first look at the baby. I was hoping it was a boy. As the picture started to come on the screen, we held each other's hand tightly, and then there was the baby. It was kind of hard to make out so the nurse described everything to us. When I saw it was a boy, I yelled, "I knew it is a boy!"

I looked at Frances and said, "You're the best, honey. I knew you could do it."

She laughed. "You did?"

"I sure did."

Frances and I had been married five years at that time. When we got married, we decided to wait five years before having a baby. We figured that would be a good time for us to get to know each other better, and if anything were to happen where things didn't work out between us, there wouldn't be any children involved. During the first five years, we had a really good time. We went out just about every weekend having fun, but now it was time to become parents and put the baby first. Frances was working for a local newspaper as a bookkeeper. I was able to bid off the midnight shift to an early afternoon shift so I could be with her at night.

I still drank and went out with the guys but not as much as I did before. The problem was when I did, most of the time I would get drunk. It seemed every time there was bad news, I used that as an excuse to drink. But that's one of the parts of the disease of alcoholism, to justify you're drinking Like the time when Frances came home and told me that she was getting laid off. We both knew it was because she was pregnant because back in those days they didn't have maternity leave like they have now. There wasn't much we could do about it. So instead of getting it together, I would go in the opposite direction.

With Frances out of work, it was hard financially; we had to pay our rent in two installments. She tried to get a job, but with her being pregnant they just didn't want to hire her. I worked as much overtime as I could get, but it still wasn't enough so I got a second job as an armored guard. Frances wasn't crazy about me carrying a gun, but I took the first job that came along. I worked there on my days off and after my regular job. We didn't see each other that often, but we did what we had to do.

The day before my twenty-eighth birthday, on the twenty-third of February 1970, we were just about to have dinner when Frances said, "I think it's time."

"Time for what?"

"For the baby."

I jumped out of my chair, grabbed the packed suitcase that we had prepared for this day, and ran out the door to head for the hospital. Trouble was that I forgot Frances! So I ran back into the house. She stood there, looking at me with a smile. "It was nice of you to come back for me."

We jumped in the car and I drove as fast as I could while she said, "Slow down, hon. You'll get a ticket."

"Okay, okay." I was so excited and nervous.

That five-mile drive seemed more like twenty miles. I think I caught every light along the way. They took her in right away to the labor room. I waited in the waiting room; little did I know it would be quite a while before she gave birth to our son. A few hours passed and they told me I could go in and be with her. I said, "Honey, do you think that since tomorrow is my birthday you could deliver him?"

She laughed. "I'll do my best."

The time was going by so slowly it seemed. She said, "Why don't you go home and get some sleep?"

"No, I'm staying here with you."

"Then at least get something to eat."

I was kind of hungry, but I was afraid to leave her. The nurse came in to check on her and told me that I could eat at the hospital cafe if I didn't want to leave. That sounded good to me so I headed for the café. I only ate a little. I wasn't as hungry as I thought. I grabbed some sleep afterward in the waiting room. When I woke up, I went back to see how she was doing and the doctor was in there. He said, "I think we're going to induce labor. It's been almost thirty-five hours."

"Can I stay with her?"

"Yes, but not for long."

When the labor pains started to come, she grabbed my hand so tight I thought she would break it. I never knew she was that strong, but I guess when you're having a baby you get super strength. She screamed so loud, "This is your fault!"

All I could say was, "I'm here, honey."

The doctor asked me to leave because it was time to deliver the baby. Back in those days, husbands weren't allowed in the delivery room. I went back to the waiting room where, at 5:17 a.m. the day after my birthday, the doctor came in and said, "Congregations, you have a healthy boy."

I shook his hand and said, "Thank you, Doc."

"Your wife told me it was your birthday yesterday. Would you like me to put on the birth certificate yesterday's date?"

I thought that would be nice, but everyone has to have his or her own birthday. "No, but thanks anyway."

I went in to see my wife, walked over to her, looked into her eyes, and said, "Thank you, honey." She looked so beautiful. She had a glow on her face like I never had seen before. It was like God himself had touched her.

A few minutes later, they bought our son to us. He was gorgeous. As I looked at him, I noticed his head seemed to look like an oval shape. I asked the nurse if he was okay. She replied, "Yes, that will go away and go back to a normal shape."

He was so precious. We looked at each other. We were so happy. Frances said, "Honey, you need to go home and get some sleep. You look so tired."

I probably was, but I was too excited and happy. I gave her and the baby a kiss and told her I would be back a few hours.

I called all our family back home and gave them the good news. Later on that day, I showed up in the hospital with a football, baseball, bat, glove, and basketball. "What are you doing, honey, with all that stuff?" my wife said.

"It's our son's presents."

"I don't believe you. He's too young for that."

"I know, but he'll have to have it sooner or later, so why not now?"

Three days later, we took him home and I gave him his first bath. As I held him in my arms, he seemed so tiny and delicate. I was afraid I would break him. We had decided to name him Thomas Francis, after my grandfather. I was the happiest guy in the world. I was a father and I wanted so badly to be the best dad I could.

A few months later, I started to drink heavily. I just couldn't seem to stop. What I didn't get at that time was I couldn't drink like a normal person and just have one or two and then lay it down. It was that I wasn't strong enough; I just didn't want to. I wasn't ready. I kept finding one excuse after another to justify it. Oh sure, I went to AA meetings, but my heart or my mind wasn't into listening to other people tell their stories and how they came to quit. What I couldn't hear was they weren't talking about themselves—they were talking to me. Just to show you how insane my thinking was after the meetings, sometimes in the middle of one I would leave and go down the street to the bar and get shitfaced because it was depressing to hear them. So I thought I'd go get happy instead.

My wife drank on occasions but not as bad as I did. She was one of those people who had a low alcohol tolerance. She could have three beers and she would have a buzz. I mean there were times she would say, "Don't you think you had enough?" but I would always have a good excuse as to why she was just imagining it.

We decided it was time to start saving for a house so we could have a place of our own. We always thought about having a house with a swimming pool. It took us a little over four years, and it was almost perfect timing since Frances became pregnant again. I asked Allan Santo, a good friend of mine at work, if he knew of anything up where he lived. "Yeah, I do,William . Why don't you come up this weekend to Newhall? We've been there for about two years and it's a great place to live."

"Sounds good. Give me the directions and we'll come up and check it out."

So that weekend, we headed up to see Allan and his wife Carmen, who we had never met; in fact, Frances had never met Allan either. They had four children: Margaret, the oldest, and then Nolan, Myra and, the youngest, Mitchell. As we drove up and got closer to Allan's place coming down into the Santa Clarita Valley on Highway 14, I couldn't believe how beautiful the scenery was: hills and trees everywhere, mountains surrounding the valley. I looked at Frances and said, "This is the place for us."

She smiled. "Yes, it's beautiful."

After our visit with Allan and Carmen, we drove back home and the very next day we contacted a Realtor to make an appointment to look at some houses there. The following week we were back there again. We probably looked at seven houses. We saw so many that we started to get confused. Then, at the last house, there it was: a three–bedroom, two-bath home with open beam ceilings, a brick fireplace, a large swimming pool, a big front yard, and a two-car garage. It was perfect, everything we wanted in a house. Now the questions were: *How much do they want for it* and *Can we afford it?*

The Realtor told us they wanted twenty-eight thousand dollars. I looked at Frances and said, "What do you think, honey?"

"It's kind of high."

"I know, but I think this would be a great place for us. The stores are close just like you wanted; the school is just two blocks away."

"Yes, but it's a long drive to work for you."

"I know, but it won't be too bad. I'm working nights so the drive will be easier and faster since there won't be a lot of traffic."

"Okay, if you think it won't be too much for you."

I gave her a big hug.

CHAPTER 7

MOVING INTO
OUR FIRST HOME

Three months later, on August 4, 1974, we moved out of Culver City to our new home in a town called Saugus in the Santa Clarita Valley. The town of Saugus had been around since the 1800s and had a lot of history, as did the rest the valley. It was about five miles from Allan and Carmen's house. Allan and I started to carpool together to work. Our son was so happy with a pool and a big yard to play in. The people who lived there before left a children's play set so it was perfect.

Six months after we moved into our new home, on February 10, 1975, at 3:17 a.m., our daughter was born. Larry, a friend from the apartments when we lived in Culver City, came up the next day to visit us. Larry, Thomas, and I went to see my wife and the baby. When we arrived at the hospital, they told us my son was too young for all of us to see so I went in while Larry stayed with Thomas.

As I entered her room, I could see my wife had that same radiant glow on her face as when she gave birth to our son. A few minutes later, the nurse bought our daughter in. I asked if I could hold her and she placed her in my arms. As I leaned toward her and gave her a kiss on her tiny face, I said, "You're Daddy's little shortcake."

My wife suggested I go back outside and bring our son to the window so he could see his new sister. I took him by his hand and said, "Let's go see your new sister at the window." He threw himself on the ground because they wouldn't let him in the room. I picked him up and he wouldn't look at me. I laughed and told him, "You can see your sister in the window."

"Put me down! I don't want to!"

After a while, when he calmed down, I took him over to the window. He started kissing the glass and saying, "My baby sister."

The hospital had given Frances an epidermal when she delivered and sat her up too soon, which caused her severe back pain. When we got home from the hospital, I had to get her into bed where she remained for three weeks. So I took my vacation to be with her and the children.

I thought taking care of the kids and cleaning house would be a walk in the park compared to work. I bathed our new daughter Elizabeth who was named after her great-grandmother. One day, as I boiled some water and put her bottle in, I went in the living room and sat on the couch and fell asleep. I was awakened by smoke. I jumped up. There was smoke everywhere. I grabbed our daughter and son, got my wife out of bed, ran outside to the neighbor's house, and yelled the house was on fire. But I didn't see any flames so I went back into the house. There was white smoke everywhere so I looked to see where it was coming from. It had a weird smell not like a fire. I went into the kitchen and there it was—the pot on the stove was smoking like crazy. I had disintegrated the baby bottle; there was nothing left. I went back over to get my wife and our children and told them what had happened. That was one time I think we must've laughed for hours. To this day we still talk about it.

About three weeks had gone by and Frances was able to get back to herself. I can tell you I'll take work over housework and taking care of children any day of the week. It was harder than my job. I felt like I was going on vacation when I got back to work.

We worked on the house, putting in a new lawn, painting the outside, and putting up a ranch-type fence. There was a plum tree in the front yard that the school kids used to pick the plums off when they were coming home from school. Those plums sure were sweet so I couldn't really blame them.

Two months passed and it was time for our daughter to be baptized. Three days before her baptism, I heated up the pool. Since it was the middle of April, it cost about a hundred dollars to heat it, and the day our daughter was baptized it hailed. The lawn was covered like a white sheet was laid on. So no one went swimming. Of all days, it had to hail, and a hundred dollars down the drain! Things were going well for us. I was still drinking but not as much. I spent a lot of time at home. My son and I would use the pool a lot in the summer and I would teach him how to swim. We would play ball in the front yard. I would teach him how to hit and throw and take him into the garage and show him how to box. Of course his mother didn't like that.

There was a local tavern down the street where they had pool leagues so one day after work I stopped in and had a few beers and inquired about the leagues. It was a small place: two pool tables and some tables and chairs lined both sides of the walls. The bar itself sat about twelve people. It was called Pete's Tavern. The locals were made up of mostly blue-collar workers, ex-cons, and other people who had brushes with the law, some serious and some not. The barmaid Helen was in her twenties, a tall dark-haired girl who like to party hard as most of the people there did. I became a regular, usually stopping in after work and on Saturdays. I joined on the leagues and we would go to other bars to compete in the pool tournaments. There were always drugs around—just about everyone on the leagues used a drug, whether it was cocaine or pot or, in some cases, heroin. Most of the beer bars in the valley were like that. I later on was offered a job by Pete to work on Saturday nights tending bar. I knew the money would come in handy so I accepted it.

As the months went by, I started to smoke pot and drink more and more heavily until it became so bad that I would spend most of my time in the bar hanging out with anyone who wanted to party. I started using Percodan, smoking pot heavily, and eating like a pig. I gained weight until I hit three hundred pounds with a fifty-inch waist. I was addicted to food, and I thought nothing of eating five sandwiches at one time. I was a mess mentally and physically, not to mention spiritually. I would go to church when no one was there and pray to God to help me. Of course, I would be drunk every time I went. Never did it sober. I would be on my knees crying and begging, I would leave church and go right to a bar where I thought I had a lot of friends, and spend money drinking and partying. I wound up taking out two mortgages on our home. Some of it would go for past bills, but most of it and whatever was left I would use to have parties or drugs. I managed to keep a lot from my wife. I handled all the finances so it was easy to hide things from her.

One day we had a big argument and she gave me a choice: her and the kids or the drinking. So in my stupid drunken stupor, I took a coin out of my pocket and said to her call it heads or tails. Tears came to her eyes, and she looked at me with pity. She said, "You need help."

I just stood there like the fool that I was, not saying a word. She turned and walked away.

The next day I called in sick to work, as I had done many times before. Only this time, I was so drunk I called in twice within an hour with two different reasons because I didn't remember calling in earlier. The next day I got a call from my supervisor who gave me a choice: go to rehabilitation or be fired. So I chose to go to rehabilitation. On December 12, 1980, my supervisor, the union representative, and the manager of the employees assistance program came to our house and spoke with my wife. She came over to me and said, "I think this is the best thing for you."

"I think it is too." I told my children that I had to go away for a while on some business for the company. Our daughter was five and our son was ten. I gave them a big hug. I knew I couldn't let them see me cry, so I gave them a big smile, kissed my wife, got into the car, and drove to the rehab center.

When we arrived, they searched me and my belongings to make sure I had no drugs or alcohol on me. I was assigned a room with a guy named Jerry. We had group counseling three times. There were about twelve of us, male and female. Things weren't easy. We had no contact with the outside world the first two weeks, and then we could have phone calls but were only limited to ten minutes.

After two weeks there, I was able to get an eight-hour pass to go home for Christmas. I called Frances and told her I would be home but just for a few hours. She replied, "That's great, honey. The kids will be so excited when I tell them."

I told her I didn't have any money but to go get the kids some presents. Two days later, when I arrived at the house about nine in the morning, I rang the bell and no one answered so I let myself in. As I entered, I saw this skimpy little tree in the corner with only two presents under it. I sat down and wondered what was going on. We always had a big tree with lots of decorations and a bunch of presents under it. Just about that time Frances and the children came home. They jumped into my arms hugging and kissing me. "Daddy, you're home! We missed you so much!" I had to tell them that it was only for a few hours and that I had to go back to work.

I took my wife in the bedroom and asked her, "How come such a skimpy tree, and where are all the presents?"

"The day you went into rehab, in the mail was over two hundred fifty dollars in bounced checks from the bank, checks you wrote for alcohol and partying, so all I had left was thirty dollars in the bank."

My heart broke right then and there and my eyes filled with tears. I felt totally emptied inside and ashamed for putting my wife and children through agony they didn't deserve.

We made the best of it that day. Frances made a nice dinner, the kids were happy, and then the time came to leave again. Leaving on Christmas night was one of the hardest things that I had to do, but I knew it was for the best, besides it was either that or lose my job.

Part of me being in rehab was that I had to complete the program. On New year's Eve, the counselors threw a party for the patients. I was sitting in my room when a few of the guys came in and asked me if I was going. I said, "No, I don't think so." I just couldn't imagine having a good time at a party without being high or drunk or both.

"Come on, go with us," one of the guys said.

After a while, I finally gave in and, to my surprise, I had a great time. I didn't think it was possible, maybe because no one was drinking.

About a week after getting out of rehab, it started: a fight inside my mind and body like that of good and evil. One side was saying, "You can have a drink," and the other side was saying, "No you can't." My body was sweating and aching for a drink. I thought when I left rehab all these feelings would go away. It became incredibly intolerable. I felt protected in rehab but now I was on my own. I fought it for as long as I could. I went to Alcoholics Anonymous meetings, where it was hard for me listening to all those people; it made me so sad. What I failed to see was I had a disease that made me sick and distorted in my thinking and actions just like they had. It was a disease that took control over my life. And then one day, on my way home from work, the evil got the best of me, what addicts call "insane thinking" or "sticking thinking." *One beer won't hurt. I can handle it. I can drink sociably.* This is some of the insanity thinking that goes on in an addict's mind.

So I went to a bar on the way home from work and only had one beer. I came out of there convinced that I was all right. After all, I said I was going to have one beer and I did. I was in control of my life; I was convinced that all I heard in rehab and in those AA meetings was bull, because if I could say I was going to have one beer and I did, then I must be right. Little did I know it would not be the last of many to come.

The disease came right back up on me, and in less than three weeks I was doing all my addictions all over again. It finally caught up with me. In one year, I was absent 147 days from work and, in June 1985, I lost my job due to my choices. Of course in my mind it was the company's fault and not mine. They were being unfair to me. What a joke! They had given me many chances to straighten up. *I've really done it this time. How am I going to tell my wife I lost my job?*

I went home that morning, walked in the house, and told her what had happened.

"Somehow we will manage," she said as we hugged each other.

Losing my job would be a blessing in disguise. I stayed away from the bars and had some money, surprisingly enough to start a small detailing business, and went to school at night to take some college courses in chemical dependency from September 1985 to February 1986. I earned two certificates in drug counseling and landed a job in a rehabilitation center, counseling children and adults until it closed its doors in September of that year. My detailing business was gone; I turned to the only thing I thought could fulfill the void deep within me: I returned to my old lifestyle.

One day, a friend of mine told me that he might be able to get me a job working for the company he was employed by. But I would have to go to get a physical first. So I set up an appointment and the following week I went for my physical. When the doctor told me I had high blood pressure, my response was, "Can I still drink and smoke?" The doctor said, "Yes, if you want to die."

When I left the doctor's office, something hit me like a ton of bricks. It was called *reality*, the reality of life; it was my love for my wife and children, and their love for me. I found the answer I'd been searching for all these years since I was a child. I was searching in all the wrong places; the answer was inside me. I had to *love myself* enough in order for me to live. What right did I have as a human being, a husband, and a father to choose to take my life away from all those who loved and cared about me? No right, absolutely none. I knew right then and there that I needed to take control of my life and accept responsibility for my actions and choices. So I left the doctor's office and threw my cigarettes in a trash can and went home.

When I arrived, I went in and changed into some sweats. I started walking a quarter mile, from home and back again, hardly being able to breathe, sweating like a pig. I thought I was going to die right then and there. That was November 13, 1986, at three thirty in the afternoon, a Thursday. I never looked back. On that day I stopped everything, meaning

I stopped doing all my addictions, everything: the drugs, cigarettes, food, and alcohol. At one time, I stopped all the things that I allowed to hold me a prisoner for so many years. That day was the first day of the rest of my life.

One of the worst things I did by my actions and choices—to drink and do other drugs—is that I abused my family, not physically or verbally but by cheating them of those years. I never went through any withdrawals or cravings like I had so many times before. What took place on that day in November was nothing short of a miracle. I think the only thing I ever did right during my years of addiction was to always love my wife and children and to encourage my children to get a good education and be at all their sporting and school events clean and sober.

I finally made a choice to take control of my life and my decisions and accept responsibility, to be accountable for my own actions. I started a new job as a mixer driver for a cement company. There were going to be many new things to come in my life that I never dreamed of.

CHAPTER 8

THE ROAD TO RECOVERY

I started to take better care of my health. I discovered race-walking. I first walked a half mile a day and then gradually increased the mileage, always taking my dog with me to keep me company. There were times when I would say, "Come on, Sparky, time to walk." And it's as if by the look on his face he was thinking, *You got to be kidding. Not again.*

I managed to work my way up to six miles a day, getting my time down to a ten-minute mile. I entered races throughout the area for two years and then, in March 1989, I entered the Los Angeles Marathon. It was my first twenty-six-mile marathon. I was really nervous. I knew the competition would be tough. Some of the best race walkers in the world were there, people who could do a seven-minute mile, but I was just hoping to finish. I even managed to get on television and be interviewed just before the race. I was becoming a celebrity! That's what I told my family. Yes, we all laughed about that one.

As I approached the starting line, I could feel my heart beat faster and the adrenaline starting to flow. The gun sounded and off we took off. There must've been over eight hundred people, mostly runners, from all over the country and the world.

I was seventeen miles into the race when I hurt my hip going around a turn. I tried to go on, but the pain was too much so I knew it would be better to stop rather than injure myself further.

I was disappointed, but I knew I couldn't let that get me down. I was determined to pick myself up and started training for the Long Beach Marathon. For the next three months, I continued to train, and in May 1989 I entered the Long Beach Marathon. I was very cautious, racing in fear that I might hurt my hip. I finished the twenty-six-mile race in six hours. I knew it wasn't a very good time, but the important thing was that I never gave up, and I finished what I started out to do.

At forty-eight and after four years of race-walking, I got burnt out and thought, *What can I do next?* I knew I had to set another goal for myself. Being an alcoholic and an addict leads to an idle mind, which is a dangerous mind.

In 1990, I took up swimming. That was always the one thing I loved even as a child. I was forty-eight years old when I started to swim in my backyard pool. I swam ten laps a day, and then overtime increased the laps until I reached one hundred and fifty, equaling a mile. It took me an hour just to go a mile in the pool. When the parks and recreation opened its twenty-five yard pools all year round, I went over there. I started out with a mile; I thought I was going to die. Big difference from the backyard pool of thirty-five feet to a twenty-five yard pool.

One day, I thought I would really like to try ocean swims. I had heard about them from other swimmers and the coach who led the master's program. My first coach was Paul, who is an accomplished swimmer. He would give us tough workouts to do. There were times I thought he just wanted to see us drown. His workouts were so hard, but I knew deep inside he was just getting us ready to compete the best we could. I remember the IMs, as we call them in the swimming world, a series of four strokes that consist of the butterfly, backstroke, breaststroke, and the freestyle. That to me was the hardest thing to do, and sometimes doing five hundred yards of them with a twenty-second rest after every one hundred yards until we were finished with the set.

Then one day I asked Greg about ocean competition. He told me there was an organization called United States Masters Swimming that I could join, and it had pool and ocean competitions all over the country. I entered my first one-mile ocean race off Santa Monica in the summer of 1990. As luck would have it, the lifeguard told me the day of the race that this was the worst current they'd had in the history of the beach and we were swimming against it. I thought, *Oh, this is just great. Will I be able to do this?* I didn't care about medals or anything, I just wanted to finish.

I got into the water and off I went, scared as I thought I would I drown out there—big difference from a pool. *Will a shark get me?* I just kept swimming while thinking, *I will do this.* And then a lifeguard came alongside me on his paddleboard and said, "You just swam in the same area three times."

The current kept pushing me back. I would go forward a yard and I'd get pushed back two. *Damn, this is crazy.* But I just kept swimming while thinking, *Nothing good lasts forever, and I hope this is good.* Well, needless to say, it came to an end. I swam toward the beach and had to run to the finish line. Thank you, Jesus, for getting me through this! I came in fourth place and received a medal.

I was so overwhelmed. To think, all I was worried about was finishing, much less winning my first ocean race medal.

Later on, I entered some pool competitions, sometimes placing first, second, or third, and sometimes dead last. I didn't care as long as I could be in the water, especially the ocean. I continued to enter ocean events, starting out with one-mile races and eventually increasing to two miles, three, six, and ten. I pushed and disciplined myself. I was working full time and swimming after work with the master's swim team at the local pool.

I remember my first three-mile swim, which was at Seal Beach. With me was my support person Olivia, who would kayak to guide me through the water and give me my feedings. I was so excited: three miles. Wow! Would I be able to make it? But I was determined to do it. Well, I did make it, even though my kayaker ran into me three times. This was her first time kayaking for a swimmer, as it was my first time doing a three-mile swim. I never had a kayaker before, so I guess you could say we were both novices. In any event, we both managed to get thorough it unharmed.

Next was my first six-mile swim. It seemed like forever. I couldn't even see the finish line. The swim took place in Goleta Beach in Goleta, California. There I met up with some of the world's best ocean swimmers. One person in particular was Jim. Here was a man who had done the English Channel and Catalina Channel. I thought, *That's the guy I'm going to ask how to swim this six-miler.* I went over to him and introduced myself. I asked, "Could you give me any tips on how to swim this race?"

He simply looked at me and said, "Just think of it as a six-mile warm-up."

Well, I did just that. The horn went off and into the ocean fifteen of us went. We swam along the pier to the end of it, turned to the left, and headed down the coast. I thought it would take me forever. Three hours and forty-seven minutes later I finished dead last, but I didn't care. I just had just swum with some of the best ocean swimmers in the world.

One thing I knew for sure was it wasn't about beating them but learning from them to become a better swimmer.

The following summer there was a ten-mile race from Huntington Beach to Seal Beach. I thought, *Why don't I do that race?* So I trained hard for several months. The first one I did was a three-miler out of Seal Beach the following week; it was the six-miler out of Goleta Beach and finally the third week the ten-miler. There we all stood at six in the morning on the shores of Huntington Beach. The waves were unusually big that morning, great for the surfers, bad for the swimmers. It would be tough getting through those waves.

The kayaker that was assigned to me had never done ocean kayaking before much less kayak for a swimmer. She had done kayaking in lakes, but that's a far cry from doing it in the ocean. It took over forty minutes for the race to get started. The kayakers kept getting turned over by the rough waves. My kayaker tried five times to get beyond the surf but it just didn't happen. Finally she just gave up. I felt so bad for her. She had no wetsuit and was freezing. The officials told me to swim out and by the time I got beyond the surf they would send me another kayaker.

When I got beyond the surf, a guy on a paddleboard came over and told me he would be my kayaker. As I swam about fifteen minutes into the race, he asked me, "How far do we have to go"

"About nine and a half miles more."

"I can't paddle that far. I have to go." And he left me.

What was he thinking leaving me there alone? I yelled to him to come back. He said he would tell the officials to send someone else. I couldn't believe this thing was so unorganized. A few minutes later they sent me two guys in a small boot. I told them I needed some fluid from my supply bag and they said, "We don't have your bag with us."

"What? Where is it?"

"We don't know."

"Well, then you need to call on the radio and tell the officials to find it and send it out to me."

Without fluids, you can dehydrate, especially when you're in a ten-mile swim. The fumes from the engine started to make me sick. The two guys in the boat were drinking beer.

I finally told them to radio the lifeguards to come and get me out. This is all I needed, two drunk guys driving a boat. When the lifeguards arrived, they helped me into their boat and took me back to shore where I was immediately put into a warm shower to prevent any hypothermia.

I was so mad at the officials for allowing this race to be nothing but a farce. They put me in harm's way. I'm just thankful nothing bad happened that day.

The following year I had heard that the same race had different officials running it and that things would be much different from the last race, so I entered it again determined to complete my first ten-mile ocean swim, This time, I had my own kayaker, an experienced woman from the San Diego Kayakers. Mary was totally organized. She had everything I needed to help me complete this race successfully. It was a hard long race; I kept thinking, *When is this going to end?* It seemed like it never would. Stroke after stroke, mile after mile, drinking fluids every half hour so I wouldn't dehydrate, I finally saw the Seal Beach pier in the distance. I never was so happy to see anything in my life. I was about two miles from the finish line.

As I continued to swim to the pier, the waters seemed to get warmer. I turned right at the pier and headed for the finish line, using the waves to help push me in closer to the shore. As I got into shore and stood up, I was wobbly. Unsteady on my feet, I struggled to keep my balance as I ran up the beach to the finish line, feeling awesome and knowing I had just completed what was one of the longest races I'd ever done.

They rushed me into a small pool filled with warm water so I wouldn't get hypothermia. After all, I was in the ocean for six hours at a temperature of sixty degrees. In July 2003, I reentered the Goleta swim. The water was about sixty-two degrees. About halfway into the swim, the winds kicked up and the ocean got pretty rough. The lifeguards had to start taking us out of the water. It was just too unsafe to continue. I climbed into the boat. I was freezing. There were no blankets. There were four other swimmers in the boat with me so we all huddle our bodies together to keep warm.

When we got to the shore, I was taken to an ambulance where I was checked for hypothermia. My body temperature had drop to ninety-two so I was rushed to the hospital where I was treated. It took over two hours to get me back to normal. I was shaking uncontrollably. That was the first time I'd experienced hypothermia, and I hope it will be the last After all I was only sixty one

A few weeks later, I was at Santa Barbara East Beach doing some training when I ran into one of the girls I swam with in the Goleta race. Jane had swum the Catalina Channel twice and was a world-class ocean competitor. She suggested I swim the channel. I said, "I couldn't swim that. It's way too far."

She said, "You can do it. I know you can."

"How long did it take you when you swam it?"

"It took me nine hours."

"I'll give it some thought."

What was I thinking? The channel, that's like twenty miles or more. I must have been crazy, but the more I thought about it over the next few months, the more it appealed to me. What a challenge that would be! I always wanted to swim the

English Channel ever since I was a kid, but since that was not possible I would do the Catalina Channel as Jane suggested. After all, it was the same distance. But why not do it so others can benefit by it. So I thought, *Who could benefit by my swim?* Then it came to me: children who are dying from cancer and other catastrophic diseases. So I went out on a mission to raise a million dollars for the Children's Research Hospital. Why them? I had people who would ask, "Why them?" and I would say, "Why not them?"

So in December 2003, I started training. I went to the pool, started out with thirty-five hundred yards a day, which is equal to two miles, and every other week I would increase it another thousand yards until I reached seven thousand yards a day, six days a week. I was swimming about twenty-four miles a week. Then in April 2004, I started ocean training off Santa Barbara East Beach, where the water temperature is about fifty-seven degrees that time of the year. The winds are high and the ocean is rough. I wore no wetsuit, just my bathing suit, goggles, and a swim cap. I went three miles the first day. It was cold and the winds were high. My wife was by my side, supporting me in every way.

We had to get up every other day at four in the morning. My wife laid out my swim gear, greasing me down before I entered the cold waters of Santa Barbara East Beach. She would be there for five to six hours, sometimes eight, making sure I was safe while I swam. She would be looking through her binoculars and watching out for me. One time, as she was looking through her binoculars, she saw two dolphins come up beside me and slow down to swim at my pace one on each side. She said if she only had a camera that day, it would've made a great picture for the newspapers. Then one crossed over my back and I could feel the smoothness of the skin. I got chills all over my body. What an experience. It is something I will never forget; it was so spiritual to be that close to two of the most beautiful creatures on earth, in the wild. I felt as if they were there protecting me.

When I finished each swim, she would bring me a towel and put it around me, and she always had a cup of hot chocolate to warm me up.

I was working a part-time job at Trader Jack's. Between the training and the job, it was taking a toll on me so I asked my boss Allen if there was any possible way I could get a leave of absence to train, but I would need somehow to keep up my medical benefits. He knew I was doing this for charity so he said he would have to check with his boss Harold, the regional vice president.

Two weeks later, Allen called me into his office and told me that my request had come through and I would get the leave of absence, with my medical benefits kept up. I thanked him for all his help and asked him to thank everyone who granted me this opportunity to complete my mission. This showed me what a really great company Trader Jack's is. They even put up newspaper articles of me throughout the store so customers could know what I was doing and put collection jars at each register to help me raise money for kids with terminal cancer and other catastrophic diseases.

It was now two thousand four and Even though I was sixty - two I kept training in the rough conditions, I got stronger and stronger both physically and mentally. Every other week I would do a fifteen-mile swim to see where I was with my training. My wife, as usual, was getting my swim gear all set up for me, rubbing Vaseline on me so I didn't chafe my skin, and wishing me well as she always did, even though she used to bring my life insurance policy with her and read it while I swam. I'm only joking! (Smile.) My wife only had a part time job and I had to draw my social security early in order to support our selves and pay for all the training and equipment , our children were grown and had families of their own.

I was swimming about 145 miles a month, four days a week. I knew I had to do a long training swim soon so the following week I entered the water for the swim with Theresa, a friend and experienced ocean kayaker who was kind enough to help me. I always would tie two twenty-ounce bottles to my waist when I didn't have a kayaker with me on my training swims. It's not good to get out of the water or to stop for too long when you swim distances in the ocean. Eight hours and twenty minutes later, I finished. *I think I'm ready for the channel.* But I knew I still had a lot of training to do.

As the days grew closer to the big swim, I wished I had more time to train. It seemed like all those days, weeks, hours, and months went by so fast. But in my own way, I was glad it was coming to a close. The training was brutal. I had no social life. I had to eat, drink, and sleep swimming, while driving 160 miles roundtrip four days a week to Santa Barbara where I swam for five or six hours, depending on the miles I would go.

I remember the day before the swim I was with my daughter. We were staying on the Queen Mary in Long Beach so I wouldn't have to travel the next day to the Dolphin, the support boat at berth 55. I had butterflies that day, thinking, *What will happen the day of the swim?* My daughter would say to me, "Dad are you nervous?" and I would just look at her as if to say, "You must be kidding me." But I would say, "What do you think?"

She would smile.

As Tuesday, September 7, 2004, arrived, I grew more nervous. It was only hours before we would be on our way to Catalina Island to cross the channel back to the mainland. At 5:00 p.m. my daughter and I arrived at berth 55 in Long Beach, where I met my son Tom, my wife who was with my daughter-in-law Roberta, and my grandchildren, D.J. and Marie. Unfortunately, my son-in-law Pedro had to work, but I knew he was pulling for me.

My son and daughter would go with me on the support boat while my wife, grandchildren, and daughter-in-law would stay on the mainland to see me come in at the finish line.

The sixty-five foot support boat was run by Captain Gregg, an experienced boat captain who had done more than sixty crossings across the Catalina Channel while guiding swimmers, and a very competent crew. They ensured the safety of the swimmers. Along with them on board is Dave the offical observer, who himself swam the Channel, and is a world-class ocean swimmer. The best kayakers were there from the San Diego Kayakers: Marty, Chuck, Don, Dave, Travis, and Pete.

As I got on the boat, the excitement began to grow. I was thinking, *There is no turning back now.* I only managed to get four hours of sleep that day.

When we left the dock, we headed over to the island. Don and Dave gave us the rules set by the Catalina Channel Swim Federation. I could not touch any part of a kayak to rest or have anyone touch me or aid me in any way. I could only wear a bathing suit and goggles and one swim cap. My fluids, which were made up of water, Gatorade, and energy powder mixed at a formula of 7 percent, had to be that amount because too much would give me cramps and to little could dehydrate me. Since my son is a mathematician, I let him handle that part.

When Dave finished explaining the rules to the support crew and me, my daughter suggested that eating something sounded good to her. My son told her that she should wait until we arrived at Catalina Island, but, being stubborn like her mom, she went ahead and ate anyhow. About an hour later she started to feel queasy and sure enough she bent over the rail and all you could hear was her gagging. She was as white as a ghost and as sick as a dog. Needless to say, she should have taken her brother's advice since the seas were kind of rough that day. I found out after the swim that she had been ill until daybreak. I lay down to try to get a little sleep. It would be a two-and-a-half-hour trip to Catalina Island.

We arrived at the island about 9:45 p.m. The reason swimmers have to swim at night is because the water is warmer, the winds are calmer, and the channel has a lot of large ship traffic during the day. You don't want to be within one hundred yards of those huge ships.

The Captain said, "We're here."

I knew I needed to get ready so I shaved my face real close to prevent chaffing of my skin. I got into my swimsuit and my children rubbed me down with Bag Balm, a gel that keeps your skin from chaffing and helps keep the water from sticking to your skin, as they joked about the rubber gloves they had to use. People were taking pictures. It was nearly time to go. The butterflies were jumping in my stomach. The tension was building. The crew put the chase boat into the water, and then Dave turned and said, "Are you ready to go, William ?"

"Yes, I am." I walked over to my children, gave them a big hug, and then turned to the crew. I shook their hands and gave my boss Allen a hug, thanking him for all he had done to get me here—if it wasn't for him, Harold, and the rest of the Trader Jack's organization, I wouldn't have been able to keep up the rigorous training it took to get me here.

As I climbed into the chase boat, everyone started to cheer. The weather was just beautiful. The water was seventy-two degrees. The air temperature was seventy-five degrees. Captain Gregg said, "Someone up there must like you. In all my crossings, I've never seen the weather so perfect."

It was very dark out—no lights anywhere. The stars filled the sky like millions of diamonds. It was gorgeous. As the chase boat left for the island to take me to the rocky beach where I would start, I surprisingly felt calm come over me. They had to shine a light on the beach so I could swim to it. It was about one hundred feet. I slid off the chase boat and swam toward shore.

I cleared the water and turned to the official. He yelled out to me, "Whenever you are ready to start!"

I looked up to the sky and said a little prayer that I would get across safely because there are great white sharks in the channel and they hunt mainly at night and early morning. I took a long, deep breath, looked up into the heavens, and moved toward the biggest challenge in my life. I could hear the sound of Captain Gregg's bagpipes as I took a step into the

Pacific. I could hear the people on the support boat cheering; it was a feeling I will never forget.

The water felt warm and it was calm as I took the first stroke and then the second, third, four, fifth, and sixth. I was trying to settle into a steady pace. I watched the water pass over my goggles like blue-green diamonds. The warmth of the water was flowing over my body as I breathed every third stroke, first on my right and then on my left.

Swimming beneath the planets and stars of the universe as they shined like diamonds above me, it got very quiet on the boat. I could see a kayak on each side of me. I had one kayaker to keep me from swimming into the support boat and the other kayaker to guide me as straight as possible. They gave me my feedings every twenty minutes. I knew there were people sleeping on the support boat.

About an hour and a half into the swim, I started to think I would like to be in a nice warm bunk right now. I knew right then and there the mind games had begun. I was told by other people who had done this swim that this was one of the worst things. You start to think negative but you have to overcome it or it would break you and you would never finish. *Stop it!* I thought. *You can't start thinking this way. Just keep swimming.*

It was beginning to get to me—maybe if I get a kink in my shoulder, then I wouldn't have to swim all the way. What if my leg cramped up? Please, God, help me stop thinking this way. It was to no avail. It wouldn't leave my mind.

This went on for hours, fighting in my mind with everything I had. Praying it would leave. The people onboard weren't allowed to eat on deck. If I had seen them eating, it would have made me hungry and I would have started to crave food, and you can't have solids in your stomach. Otherwise you will cramp.

As I swam, I started to feel the stinging, first on my hands and then on my arms, face, and back. I knew what it was: jellyfish floating in the ocean. Hundreds of them. Even though tentacles break off from the animal, they can still sting you. As I swam through them, I could feel the burning and stinging. This went on for about three hours.

I knew I couldn't stop. If I did, I would surely give in to my thoughts so I kept swimming, stopping every twenty five minutes to take on liquids for about fifteen seconds. To do so, I rolled over on my back, kicking my feet so I could drink, then I was off again swimming, thinking, *When will I see the break of day? How long have I been swimming? It seems forever. How many strokes am I doing a minute? Is my form good? Are my strokes strong enough? Am I reaching out far enough? Am I rotating my shoulders the way I'm supposed to, as I come up on my left side for air? I can see the lights on the support boat and the kayaker. It's so quiet on the boat. I see some people but I can't make out whom they are. The moon is blood red and looks so huge. Are my children watching? What are they thinking about?*

Then as I looked up, I saw the very slightest change in the sky. *Is it a break of day or my imagination? I can see the sky. The stars are still there. I'll swim some more and look later. What time is it? Should I ask? Do I really want to know?*

As I looked up one more time, yes, it was turning to daylight and all of a sudden the feelings of quitting left me as I thought, *I'm not going to quit. I can do this. I must do this.*

I began to swim like I was born to be there. The stars started to disappear. The moon faded away, the day became brighter, and the sun started to rise in the east. Everyone onboard came up from the lower decks cheering. I could hear my daughter shouting, "You can do it, Dad! You can do it!"

I felt the spirit of God fill my head with positive thoughts! It was a beautiful day for a swim. I could now see the cliffs of Palos Verdes in the distance. They looked so far away. Then I remembered what Cathy, the woman who had swum it before me, told me: "Don't look at the cliffs." I kept my eyes closed from them, and I swam and swam and swam. The captain and all the other wonderful people were there to help and support me.

I could feel the ocean starting to get rough. I could feel the change in temperature of the water. It had been getting colder somewhere around 8:00 a.m. The water had dropped to sixty degrees. I had to speed up my strokes to get my heart level up higher to keep me warm. The winds were kicking up. I thought, *How bad can this get?* I know I had trained long and hard in rough waters in case something like this happened, but I kept pushing. I knew I was close to completing my dream.

When I was about six miles from shore, the kayakers beside me, Chuck and Dave, were saying, "You're doing great! We're almost there." Dave would say, "Your stroke is long and strong."

I was a little bit tired by then. I kept saying in my mind, *Nice and easy, nice and easy.*

Finally I stopped again for my feeding. "How many more feedings do you think I'll need, Dave?"

"I think about eight more feedings. After that, you should be on land."

I put my face in that ocean and I swam hard, fighting the rough waters that the winds had kicked up. I could feel myself getting tossed around like a ball swells which are like rolling hills only with force behind them hitting me in the face. When I would come up for air, trying not to swallow half the ocean.

After three hours of this, I looked up again. I was within one hundred feet of the beach!

Dave guided me in. There are only rocks along the cliffs. I had to be very careful landing; the ocean waves could smash me into the rocks. I had to try to time the waves. I followed Dave's instructions, and he got me into the safest spot possible. I had to climb out on all fours. The rocks were extremely slippery as I climbed up, doing it carefully on hands and knees.

Then a wave came behind me and pushed me onto the other rocks with such force. I was pushed about ten feet onto the rocks, slamming my right thigh into them. I continued to crawl, knowing that I had to get out before another wave came. I was slipping. I couldn't stand. It was impossible. I was bent over. I had to clear the water and wait for the official to give me the signal that I was clear and that it was over.

Since I couldn't stand up, I looked between my legs and saw the official. He gave me a touchdown sign: two hands in the air, meaning I cleared the water and I successfully swam the Catalina Channel!

I turned and sat down, put my head on my knees, and wept. I could hear the horn blowing from the boat and

Captain Gregg playing his bagpipes. The people on the cliffs were yelling and cheering. All the people in the boat were waving their arms. I was so excited.

I knew I had to get back to the chase boat because the winds had come up and I was getting cold. I slid down the rocks and into the ocean and swam to the chase boat where my son and daughter helped me into the boat; they had me lie down on the bottom of the boat to keep me out of the wind as much as possible.

As I lay there, shivering, my daughter turned to my son and said, "Take some pictures of Dad."

I could hear my son say, "What's wrong with you? This is Dad's worst moment and you want me to take pictures of him shivering?"

I just lay there and started laughing as we headed back to the support boat.

They wrapped me in plastic bags to help prevent hypothermia from setting in. The shivering subsided when I got onboard and they had me take a lukewarm shower and checked me over to make sure I was okay.

We went back to berth 55 in Long Beach where my friends, family, and reporters from the ABC affiliate, Channel 7, were all gathered on the dock. My grandson D.J. and my granddaughter Marie ran up to me and jumped into my arms, kissing and hugging me. My heart filled with joy as I walked over to my wife and kissed her. We both began to cry.

I think there were tears everywhere that day. Afterward, we did an interview with the media.

For days after the event, I still couldn't believe I swam the Catalina Channel. I spoke to Dave one night and told him how I felt. He suggested I go down to Point Vicente and look out across the ocean at Catalina Island. So I did just that the following Sunday. My wife and I approached the point in the town of Palos Verdes and parked our car. I thought, *What will I feel when I see the island?*

We walked out to the point and looked out across the blue Pacific and how huge it was. I saw Catalina and it hit me like a ton of bricks. *I have accomplished what only a few people in the world have done.* The very first was in 1927 and I was the 107th person in 2004. Many people have tried, and few have made it. To be in the same company with some of the finest ocean swimmers in the world is an honor.

My time for the swim was thirteen hours nonstop. I later found out I was the second-oldest person to swim the channel.

That day, I thought as I looked across the ocean about the wonderful people who made it all possible, the real winners and true athletes in their own right: the children who are fighting every day of their lives and praying for a cure. Not just for those kids who I did this for, but for all the children around the world.

I lived with shame and fear most of my life because of the things that happened to me when I was a child. I had no control over those things. There was no help, there was no one I could tell without feeling shame and living in fear of what people would say.

Never let shame or fear stop you as I did. You have the means today. There's help out there.

I hope this book has helped you, even if it is in a small way. I know it has helped me by telling you my story. It has taken away the shame and the fear that have haunted me for many, many years. Remember: better late than never.

We must look into ourselves to find the truth of who we truly are and what we can be. Know that loving yourself is okay, because if you can't, how can you love others who love you? We as a people need to share the wonderful gifts of who we are and what we have to offer to make this a better world. And if you do this, I promise your life will be a joy and you will overcome.

There's a song called "If I Can Dream" and some of the words go like this: "We're caught in a cloud with too much rain, we're lost in a world with too much pain, but as long as a man has the strength to dream, he can redeem his soul and fly, he can fly. If I can think, if I can stand, if I can walk, if I can talk, then why can't I make my dream come true right now?"

If it were not for my family and friends who have supported me with love and encouragement, I would never have fulfilled the dream I had as a child.

The End. *No.*

The Beginning? Absolutely.

I hope you will find something in this poem, which I gave to my wife, to make your life a little bit happier.

Oh, Please Remember

I leave this thought with you my love.

If I should go away,

From time to time drift into dreams

About our bygone day,

Dwell for awhile on tender times

A glow with happiness, then

Close your eyes and you will feel

The warmth of my caress.

Death never can erase true love.

It only makes it stronger.

So roam

The land of reverie and

I will linger longer.

Inside my heart

You'll

Always be in life's spring or December.

I leave this thought with

You, my love, that says

Oh, please remember.

I wanted to share with all my readers this poem that was given to me by my daughter in two thousand seven on my sixty-fifth birthday. I hope you all enjoy.

Daddy, You've Come a Long Way

From a baby to a child
To a boy to a teenager
To a man to someone's boyfriend
To someone's husband to someone's father
To someone's grandfather.
From a drug addict and alcoholic to a Christian.
Finally you have become every daughter's thought
Every daughter's wish
Every daughter's dream.
You have become her number one hero,
Always thinking and giving
To everyone before giving to yourself.
You help when no one else would.
You help become
A swimmer
A fundraiser
and a volunteer.
You have become my sunshine on a cloudy day.

You are my light when I can't find my way.

You are my inner soul when times are tough.

You are my daddy and all of this is why

I love you so much.

I am proud of you in all that you are,

In all that you do.

You are my world.

I love you, Daddy.

You've come a long way.

CPSIA information can be obtained
at www.ICGtesting.com
Printed in the USA
BVHW081700240223
659183BV00015B/768